Aleksandar Krzavac

I0152503

Media Guy

God Blesses Media,
but not Media Professionals

Editions Dedicaces

MEDIA GUY.
GOD BLESSES MEDIA, BUT NOT MEDIA PROFESSIONALS

Published by:
    Editions Dedicaces LLC
    12759 NE Whitaker Way, Suite D833
    Portland, Oregon, 97230
    www.dedicaces.us

Library of Congress Cataloging-in-Publication Data
    Krzavac, Aleksandar
    Media Guy. God Blesses Media, but not Media Professionals /
      by Aleksandar Krzavac.
    p. cm.
    ISBN-13: 978-1-77076-425-5 (alk. paper)
    ISBN-10: 1-77076-425-9 (alk. paper)

Aleksandar Krzavac

Media Guy

God Blesses Media,
but not Media Professionals

Chapter 1

Small, but modern downtown discotheque. Multicolored light show. In the center is dance floor. Around dance floor small tables are located, each with lamp. Some people are sitting, others dancing.

There are no lots of people in discotheque. Atmosphere is very pleasant. Johny, Media Guy steps dance floor, holding microphone tight. Other people leave dance floor surrounding Media Guy; they make circle around him.

Media Guy starts singing and dancing. Although not so professional as David Bowie or Michael Jackson Johny alias Media Guy attracted attention of almost all visitors that hot summer night. At that point discotheque attendants get more cheerful and focused to not so talented singer and dancer.

Media Guy was singing and dancing trying to do something that he is not capable to do. He acts as if he is clown all time he is singing song. Johny makes funny faces, moving knees and whole body left-right, shaking his head, opening his mouth wide, showing nice snow-white teeth. His dancing is extremely dynamic. Other people are much more astonished by his dancing efforts than with his dancing skills. His hips are swinging, eyes rolling. Extraordinary efforts to make dance and singing outstanding make audience believe that lack of talent could be compensated by hard work. That is the cast with Johny.

Song Lyrics:

My mother told me: "You must be Media Guy"
My mother told me: "You must be Media Guy"
In this damned world there is nothing
valuable to try
than to be
Media Guy

My father told me:
"No greater happiness for your mother and me
than to see you on TV"

My father told me:
"No better vision
than to be on television"

Auuhhh…Ohh…Auuhh…Ohh…Auuhhh…Ahh…
Girls hearing I'm employed with TV
No matter, whether blondes, brunettes or reds
promptly saying to me:
Let's go to beds

Auuhhh…Ohh…Auuhh…Yooppie…
Auuhhh…Yooppieee…
Socialism…Capitalism…Altruism…
Germanism…Americanism…
No…For sure, no any ism…
but journalism…

Ohh…Aauuhh…Aauhh…Yeahh…

I am a star
I am Media Guy
Bye, bye, bye

Finishing the song Media Guy stretches out right hand with microphone towards group of his new "fans" in discoteque. He was completely soaked by sweat as if he was running at Olympic Games. He is acting as if he makes interview with camera. Sweat drops were rolling down his face, he was almost flat out.

Media Guy tries to ask typical, boring bullshit question looking at group of his "newborn fans" standing next to him "Mister! Miss! Please, could you tell us something about...?!?" He stopped for a moment continuing "About this stageshow dance show".

Chapter 2

Ordinary editorial office of an electronic media – in this case USFTV – United States Future Television. There are lots of journalists doing their job – preparing news. Some of them chat or drink coffee and hot chocolate. Generally speaking, high intensity working environment.

Office of Editor in chief is separated by thick glass. Media Guy, rather tall, slim man, age of 40 or so, talks to Editor in chief, good looking gentleman at age between 50 and 55.

Editor in Chief sitting in luxurious black CEO style armchair, looking at some papers talks to Media Guy "Hmm... Here it is..." raising his head, starts looking at Media Guy. "This is really good assignment for you... Well...Now... Small bridge should be opened in Knoxtown, tomorrow morning. I don't know exact time... But check it. You are journalist. Do some investigation", said Editor in Chief to Media Guy.

Media Guy is istening to Editor in chief carefully, simply absorbing each single word "Yes, Sir... Just take it's already done..." Editor in chief keeps talking "For sure... That's not Golden Gate"... smiling "But"... Editor makes very short break starring to Media Guy "What's the most important is that... construction of the bridge was financed by local community. We must emphasize that fact. In particular today when Tax evasion becomes the general rule from small local communities up to Congress, and even White House"

Media Guy gets a little bit confused and frightend, probably, due to his journalistic inexperience. His look was very anxious, face got pale. He muttered taking some air and sighed "Hmm... I see... Well... Okay"

Editor in Chief talks " Yeah... I guess there will be some local officials... Important people to community. Make interview with them. Do not come here without some interview or, at least, brief a couple of lines comment"

Media Guy's face has got natural color again, as he got rid of any fear. "Of course... That would be blockbuster interview, believe me", replies Media Guy.

Editor in Chief looks suspicious "Please don't exagge-rate... We must... I mean our TV boost moral of young people doing patriotic way... Yeahh..." nodding his head "Last night I saw commercial with U.S. flag on condom... Awful... And the same. Flag of our country painted on naked girl's ass... What craps... That is not creation, but misuse of democracy"

Media Guy bursting in laughter "Hmm, Doesn't matter...In particular if lady's ass was nice... What about painting US flag on women pubic parts? "

Editor in Chief getting annoyed with such statement, trying to pretend as if he didn't heard "What, What did you say ?!? The authors of such bullshit should be prosecuted... Now, Leave the office... Go !!! Go to that bridge... And don't screw it up..."

Media Guy was a bit ashamed while leaving Editor in Chief office. He remembered wise words of his father "Use your head to think not to grow your hair. Do not speak before thinkining".

Chapter 3

Knoxtown. People are gathered to celebrate bridge opening. There are around 500 citizens. Bridge is small, but very important to that community. Besides Knoxtown citizens, there were several TV crews and some local politicians. Crowd is on Knoxtown side of the bridge. Happy people are waiting grand opening. Knoxtown Mayor prepares himself to make a speech. Media Guy is standing several feet from the bridge on pavement. His face is cheerful, his eyes look straight at camera, microphone is gripped by his hand.

"Hello. Ladies and Gentlemen. You are looking USFTV …Live coverage of the bridge opening. Stay tune…" says Media Guy at his first report.

At that point bridge suddenly starts trembling. People are shocked. Gradually bridge trembling becomes shaking. Crowd on the bridge starts sudden rush towards the city.

Media Guy seeing there won't be any bridge opening, what exactly is his assignment, tells cameraman to turn off the camera, suggesting to step aside and buy some beverage in cafeteria located nearby the bridge. USFTV Crew starts calm walking to cafeteria as if nothing has happening. Camera and microphone are turned off.

Panic-stricken people reach solid ground leaving the bridge; but most of them keep running to get further as

11

possible from the bridge. Very loud, horrible sound is heard. Bridge collapsed into river. During getaway from the bridge, some people fallen. Fortunately, nobody is seriously hurt.

Cameraman speaks to Media Guy: "Don't you think we should take several shots of collapsed bridge and panic-stricken people? It could be interesting for audience. Scene is pretty unusual, rare to be seen".

Media Guy replies sharply: "Oh, no... Not at all... Not in any case...

Editor in chief told me to shoot the bridge opening not bridge collapsing into river...Is that clear to you! That's none of your business, you are only cameraman, not journalist."

Chapter 4

Editor in chief office. Media Guy is back. Editor in chief is furious, walking aimlessly, making circles around his table; from time to time he stops next to the window starring outside. Media Guy figures out that something terrible has happened. Sitting in the chair He looks crushed as if he is waiting for verdict. But it seems late now to correct the mistake.

Editor in Chief, still furious, walking in the office, screams at Media Guy:

"Nothing!!! Nothing has happened... Oh, Jesus, what idiot you are! Bridge collapsed into the river and nothing has happened!!! Oh, my Lord..." He is putting hands on his head, disappointed as never so far. Sound of deep sighing is heard.

Media Guy is really frightened, his face is totally pale, speaking through clenched teeth: "Bb... Bb... But... But... Wh, Wha.. What happened?"

Editor in Chief, cannot control himself keeps screaming at Media Guy:

"No! No but... That's me who is dumb...You know why!?! Because I hired you!!!Yeah, I am complete idiot, not you".

Media Guy, frightened and silent has no idea what to reply: "But... But you told me... Don't you remember what you told me?"

Editor in Chief, still very angry and loud speaks both to Media Guy and likely himself: "What about my reputation? Other media broadcast – USFTV hasn't any news...Or, at least, a single shot of bridge collapsing into the river. Shit".

Media Guy still frightened tries to help Editor in Chief and finally himself: "So... Please, tell me what to do to improve our rating?

Editor in Chief still loud, but not screaming any more: "What to do!?! You, dumb, ask me what to do. To fire stupid journalists... Journalists like you. That's the only way out..."

Obviously shocked Media Guy bursts in sudden crying, tears are sliding down his pale face: "No... Please, don't do it I beg you..."

He puts his hands as if he asks for forgiveness. "I don't know what other job I could do...And... Finally my parents, in that case, would disown me... They think journalism is the only job worth doing..." tells Media Guy sobbing.

Editor in Chief is taking pity on him. "Okay, okay... Take a week vacation... It's better for both of us... I'll call you... Now, Get Lost... 1,2,3 (counting) Have you heard me? GGGet Lost of my office !!!", says Editor in Chief almost screaming.

Media Guy is getting out of chair and leaves the office quickly feeling very ashamed and unhappy.

Chapter 5
Eight days later

Media Guy is preparing meal for him and his girl, Susan, who is sitting at dining table in dining room of hired apartment. Atmosphere is pleasant. Media Guy is cheerful; reason is free night to make pleasure to his beloved girl.

Media Guy is singing cheerful song in the kitchen. Loudly to his girl:

"Honey, do you like fish fillets with or without ketchup?"

Susan replies in pleasant, sweet voice of young lady: "As you like it… Doesn't matter… It's up to you… I need you whole evening and night". She starts smiling and sighing.

Media Guy gets very touched by her words: "Oh, Honey… I'm coming within few minutes…"

Susan is thrilled, her heart is trembling, feels jitters: "Oh, Sweetheart… I am waiting for you…"

Media Guy is finishing meal for two. He is not five star cook but in such cases he exceeds even own expectations.

"Just to put dressing… You know… Some sauce on fish fillets. Oh… I almost forgot… To make pomfritte…", explains Media Guy to his beloved girl.

CD player is turned on; nice evergreen music for people in love is heard. After a while Media Guy is entering dining room with meal, comes to dining table and serves it. (After finishing serving Media Guy sits at dining table).

Media Guy with mouth wide smiling: "Let's go straight to the point!"

He and his girl start eating the meal.

"Hmmm... This is delicious. Real masterpiece of cooking...", says Susan.

Media Guy cannot believe how good cook he has just become, confirms in shy voice: "I agree... This is not bad... Hmm, it might be even excellent"

Susan smiling shows her happy face: "You'll be awarded after meal...Guess what your reward is!?!", looks at him "eye to eye focus".

"That's me. The very best prize you can win", says she smiling.

Media Guy choking up suddenly, very thrilled and happy eager to pass very soon happenings with his girl: "Oh... Do you mean... We will make love?"

Susan looks at him with erotic sensual smiling: "Yeah, that's it. Exactly... What a smart guy you are..."

Media Guy starts stammering from huge and sudden inflow of excitement:

"We... We... will... be... naughty... Very naughty... Is that so?

Susan replies still smiling: "Yeah...You are right... Keep eating I'm impatient... We'll do X-rated stuff... My naughty boy".

Media Guy, now gets very cheerful, speaks very loudly: "Our bodies as well our souls will be the one... We'll make love... At dining table... In bathroom or... Balcony... Why not? Yoopieee..."

At that point his mobile phone is ringing. He takes mobile phone very nervously.

"Bullshit, who is it", says he to himself. "At this point, and this night I don't need anybody but you, Susan", says Media Guy to his girl.

Media Guy speaks over mobile phone: "Yeah... I see... Yeah".
On other side is his Editor in chief.
Editor in Chief over phone, rather nervous: "Urgent stuff. There is a big fire in downtown area... Just go... Go there immediately... Do you understand. GO IMMEDIATELY".

Media Guy gets furious, his face turned red, angry look as if he would smash person on other side of the phone line. He speaks over mobile phone: "Shit! No chance...I must have some days and nights off...Especially nights! Do you happen to know, dear gentleman, what Human Rights and Freedom Act are!!!"

Editor in Chief over phone very angry: "Hey, hey Guy... Listen to me carefully... You'll do this assignment or... You'll be fired... I promise you I'll fire you if you don't come to fire site within half an hour... And... (pause) Please, never, never act as if you are movie star! You are still nothing, or almost nothing. Sorry, just entry level journalist. IS THAT CLEAR."

Obviously phone talk is interrupted suddenly. Editor in Chief didn't want to keep talking that way to Media Guy. Beep signal is heard

Chapter 6

Downtown area, night sky is clear but around building in fire is very smoky. Therefore people can't see each other clear. There are many Fire Department, police and ambulance vehicles on parking lots near building in fire. Red flame over central part of building looks threatening. Sirens of emergency vehicles and fire sputtering are heard. Firemen try to extinguish or at least prevent fire from spreading. Big black smoke makes people coughing. Rescue squad tries to help people inside building; fortunately there are no people in building. Some firemen and Rescue squad people are with masks.

Of course, journalists are unavoidable in such cases– there are several TV crews "on site" of the event. Sometimes media professionals are faster than Fire Department and ambulance. The faster media, the better reports, and, of course bonuses as rewards for hard work.

Media Guy holding microphone, his eyes look straight at camera, tries to be calm although rather upset: "Hello, ladies and gentlemen… You are looking USFTV… Live Coverage… Unfortunately, the big fire in downtown area ALIVE… Stay tune… "

Media Guy holding microphone, speaking directly to camera: "Hi… We'll try to go to the very heart of happening… Building caught by fire… Let's go!"

He is waving his hand, points at building in fire. Media Guy and cameraman start risky operation – entering building in fire. On his way they are pushing policemen and guys from security agency just to reach the building that is blocked all-round. Some ten feet from entrance door two big policemen are standing.

Policeman 1 to Media Guy in threatening voice: "Hey, hey! You cannot go further! Stay where you are! Or..."

Media Guy replies and acts as if he didn't hear anything: "What! No chance... I must go in!"

Policeman 2 threatening voice to Media Guy: "You must obey the rules! Otherwise you'll be arrested...this is Police Department! And who are you?"

Media Guy gets very nervous and angry wasting his time in communication to cops: "Shit! Media is allowed to go anywhere...That's our job too, not only yours."

Policeman 1 very angry to Media Guy: "Hey... Listen to me carefully! You... and cameraman have five seconds to leave this point! I'm start counting... (pause) 1... 2... 3..."

Media Guy and cameraman look at policemen as if they say nothing. Actually, all four are very confused.

Policeman 1 still counting: "4... 5... 6..."

At that point Media Guy hits policeman 1 and cameraman hits policeman 2 into face so strongly that both policemen fall down. After that Media Guy and cameraman break into building in fire. Entering building Media Guy and cameraman at that point realize they risk, even, their lives. Smoke and fire are all-round them. It's very difficult to breathe the air; burnt ceiling and floor parts are falling. Although panicky Media Guy is locating himself to start TV report (Live coverage). Cameraman takes more secure position some 10 to 15 feet from Media Guy.

Media Guy trying to hide he is frightened to death, look straight to camera lens:

"Hello again! USFTV Live Coverage of downtown fire continues! Stay tune, please." At that point sudden crack is heard and Media Guy disappears falling through hole made by fire.

Chapter 7

Media Guy is the only injured person in fire in downtown area. Due to falling through hole made by fire he got broken leg and some serious scratches and bruises on his body. He has strong pain in his muscles and arms. However, he is pride of himself. He is hero. Now, he is in City hospital, not badly injured, but it will take couple of months to get the old shape. Almost whole his body; except head, neck and chest is wrapped in bandages. His broken leg is in cast hanged up.

Editor in chief with huge chocolate in his hands is looking for the room where Media Guy lies. Hospital corridor is full of medical staff, patients and visitors.

Finally, he finds room where Media Guy is.

Editor in Chief entering room, cheerful, tries to comfort Media Guy by tapping him on right shoulder. He speaks loudly to injured journalist: "Hi, Hero! Good boy, god journalist and… First of all and after all good man. How are you?"

Media Guy starts coughing and choking; painful, speaks to Editor in Chief:
"Ouch! For the Christ sake, what are you doing?!? I am half of man… You'd better don't look at me".

Editor in Chief suddenly ashamed, apologizing to injured journalist: "I am sorry… I am awfully sorry… I know you like sweet stuff…" He makes short pause. "So… I bring you a chocolate…" He puts chocolate on small shelf next to Media Guy. Proud of Media Guy Editor in chief continues: "Your live fire coverage is... believe me... The best ever seen on USFTV so far..."

Media Guy, not so happy by Editor in chief state-ment, seems ironic: "Yeah... Due to your best live coverage I am almost dead... What for!?! For your career and your profit... Yeah... My boss... My leg is broken, body full of bruises and scratches. For the sake of your live coverage. Shit..."

Editor in chief not accustomed to see Media Guy angry, tries to calm him:
"Okay... Okay... Please, don't blame me." He is nodding his head, tries to comfort him: "You are the winner... Forgive me for all I have said to you... Please..."

Media Guy looks annoyed with such way of talking, not sure is that honest statement or just cynical phrase editors use in such occasions: "Okay... I forgive you... But promise... You shall never... never threaten me by firing". He makes small pause shifting his look from the editor's face to his broken leg.

Media Guy continues speaking to his Editor in Chief: "Have you heard me? Never honor me by firing... NEVER."
Editor in Chief sharply replies: "I promise... You have my word... I was terribly wrong about you. Forgive me. And... Is there anything more you would like me to do?"
Media Guy speaks sharply in voice full of self-confidence: "Of course... Yes... To raise my salary... It's to low. I cannot afford decent life".
Editor in Chief: "Sure... Take it's done...How much?
Media Guy continues: "Twice..."

Editor in Chief shocked, starts stammering: "Ttt... Tw... Twi... Twice... Please could you reduce your will... Let's say... 70 per cent... Hmm... I guess it's enough".

Media Guy now gets very serious and persistent: "No... No chance... Twice that... or nothing... Otherwise I'll find other TV company that appreciates talent and work... He acts now as if he is the boss to Editor in Chief, speaks loudly and sternly to him: "I guess, I was quite clear about mentioned... Clear!"

Editor in Chief cannot refuse him, reluctantly: "You... Movie Star... All right... All right... You got 100 per cent up..."

Chapter 8
Seven weeks later

Media Guy healed and restored, now, feels good. He is with his parents in their small, but nice family house. They all are sitting at the table in dining room eat and chat. There are several dishes on the table as if it's prepared for some kind of celebration. However, despite that atmosphere is rather tense.

Father while eating to Media Guy: "Where are you? You haven't been here to visit your parents for more than seven months…"

Mother is trying to stop talking about that: „Hey, don't talk that way to our son! He is journalist… Extremely busy… Don't you understand…"

Media Guy with full mouth, talks to father taking mother's side swallowing food:

"Yeah… No… No, for sure… No chance you can understand what means to be employed with TV… Non stop on alert".

Father surprised with such reaction tries to avoid possible conflict: "Okay… All right… But… Hmmm, I'm not quite sure you are so busy you cannot visit us for one day… We don't live on Hawai. That's long distance, not this".

Media Guy replies to father: "That's your problem… Believe me or not… That is not ordinary 9 to 5 office job… It is as if you are in the mill… Job called trouble."

Father at that point seeing bad side of journalism, to Media Guy; mother is just watching both of them without taking part at that point: "Yeah... You are maybe right... Whole my life I've worked as office clerk..." Father makes deep sad sigh: "Working hours 9 to 5... An hour break for lunch... Hmm."

Father obviously unsatisfied with own life continues: "Quite anonymous... And... I've dreamed whole my life to become famous... To see my name on TV... or... at least in some well known journal...But, my dreams have never become the true... But... You, my son... You are famous... You are journalist employed with TV."

Media Guy worried about his father tries to comfort him: "Believe me... There is nothing to regret for... Finally, you had some kind of order in your life..." He is talking as if he complains about his job: "Do you happen to know... Hmm... How many times I've been interrupted while being in cinema or theatre, or sitting on toilet bowl or even making love. And... Always was urgent... Order is – Go immediately... Yeah".
It looks now as if Media Guy envies his father on his job
Father still sad and disappointed about himself, his job and his life in general:
"But you are famous... I've worked for forty years... And nobody knows me... That's really terrible."
Desperate Father talks: "I started my career as nobody... And I retired as nobody...".

Mother trying to change the topic for atmosphere that obviously becomes unpleasant, even sad: "Hey, hey, guys let focus you to this great selection of dishes..." She is pointing at the table, wide smiling.

Media Guy approving mother's idea, cheerful: "Yeah... It's high time. Let's go eating, stop wasting time... Dishes are getting cold..."

Father looks as if he is accepting less boring stuff and gradually gets cheerful:

"Anyway... My son carried out my dream... Dream of becoming famous, well-known personality to millions of people."

Deep sighing comes out father again.

Mother and Father together in one voice: "Our son... We are pride of you... Lucky us."

Media Guy makes his ordinary official wide, wide smile: "I have never doubt about it...In addition you were and you stay up to nowadays my great support..."

After debate on sense of life and comparing jobs, finally, they focus to food starting intensive eating and stop chatting.

Chapter 9

Media Guy is sleeping in bedroom of his apartment. His sleeping is rather noisy – he snores loudly. Telephone located on the small carpet on the floor next to bed starts ringing. It's long ringing – 5 or 7 times. Media Guy awaken up hesitates to take receiver, then tries to take it, but drops couple of times. Finally, he takes receiver. Sleepy and angry due to interrupted sleeping.

Media Guy over phone: "Yeah... Yeahh... Who are you?"

Unknown person over phone, strange voice, onomatopoeia. Media Guy hears animals in ZOO, or something similar to those sounds.

"Uuuu... aaaaa..wwww............ rrrrrrr............ bbbbbbbb... OOOhhh......................"

Media Guy rather confused over phone: "No... No... You are wrong!!!" He is putting receiver back in telephone hand set. "Shit", this city is full of lunatics. I must sleep" he says to himself. He is trying to continue sleeping, but seeing on wall clock that time is 11 a.m. Media Guy gets out and starts making the bed. All time he is whistling and makes funny faces.

Media Guy each single day after getting out of bed he feeds his pets: first-small tropical fishes in aquarium, then nice parrot in bird cage. Approaching to aquarium, talks fishes he says: "Hi. Girls... How is today?".

While talking he is dropping fish food in aquarium then puts his point finger in water. He says: "Oh... You are so nice but mute... I am leaving you... I'm looking for someone who will talk with me."

He is going to birdcage. Cheerful, greets parrot: "Hi... Friend of mine. What about you... How are you today?"

Parrot is able to talk some words – more precisely, dirty words.

"Craps only... Craps only... Shits all around us"

Green parrot is happy to see Media Guy, continues with his vocabulary: "Fuck the world... Fuck the world... Fuck media."

Media Guy smiling and putting parrot food in special dish hanged on birdcage. He is proud and ashamed of parrot speech at same time.

"Shame on you... You, little bastard.", said Media Guy smiling.

Parrot repeats his words and continue speaking: "Shame on you... You, little bastard. Fuck the world... Fuck the media... Fuck the journalism... Journalists too... Craps... Craps... Craps..."

Media Guy after finishing feeding his pets leaves for bathroom to prepare him for new day. After face washing and teeth brushing Media Guy takes off his pajamas and takes shower. Almost all time washing his face and teeth brushing he looks at bathroom mirror making funny faces, showing his teeth, moving and sticking out tongue as well as rolling eyes. Media Guy looks very, very funny at those moments. After he puts on shower curtain and adjusts shower jets optimal Media Guy starts taking shower. Of course, now he is singing and whistling too. Melody is easy, his singing funny.

Toothpaste, toothbrush, soap, aftershave lotion etc… And, surely, there is his mobile phone… Nowhere with that gadget. Mobile phone is ringing. He is trying to take mobile phone from small bathroom shelf. He slipped pulling shower curtain and fell. Wrapped in shower curtain Media Guy is lying on bathroom floor. He speaks over mobile phone: "Yes… Yes… Okay…"

Editor in Chief over mobile phone: "Hurry up… You must be within an hour in USFTV Headquarters to interview British Minister of Health…"

Media Guy happy with this new assignment proudly over mobile phone: "Okay. Take it's done. I am coming"

Jesus, Minister of Health, that's first VIP I will interview, thinks Media Guy putting on his best suit for special occasions.

*

Chapter 10

On his way to USFTV Headquarters streets are crowded by cars. Media Guy is in hurry, very nervous waiting for green light at semaphore. He fidgets in his car looking at rearview mirror making his hair using hands and small comb. As usual when looking at mirror he makes funny faces – smiling, showing teeth…

Media Guy gets very nervous, looking at traffic lights, to himself: "Green. Shit. Where is that bloody green light !?!"

There is clock display at semaphore. It shows 5 seconds to green light. No, he cannot stand waiting longer. He starts driving through red light. Due to sudden acceleration sound of squeaking of wheels is heard. Barely avoided accident his car passed through intersection at red light. But, by this irresponsible action of not obeying traffic rules he caused, or at least, contributed to collision of seven cars, which were going through green light. *Doesn't matter*, he thinks, *I passed through intersection*. Satisfied due to avoiding collision, deep sigh of relaxation as a sign of escaping danger comes out his mouth.

Media Guy wipes drops of cold sweat from his forehead increasing speed: "Uuhh, lucky me".

He drives vehicle very fast through the city speaking to himself: "Jesus! What time is it?". He focus his eyes on his watch. He got scared seeing what time it is. He criticizes himself loudly in vehicle cabin: "Oh... Shit... I must be in studio within three minutes! Shit... Oh, no. No way. I must not be late!"

Media Guy is switching on car radio adjusts sound to high level. Sound of music, full of rhythm is heard. He is speaking to himself worried: "Hurry up! Hurry up!".

Finally, Media Headquarters; Media Guy parked his car on parking lot next to main entrance, gets out and start running towards studio.

Security officer at the entrance smiling: "Hurry up! Hurry up! Keep your job Media Star! Pardon...Superstar!"

After short running through the corridor Media Guy reaches studio. He is late about 90 seconds. British Minister of Health is there sitting in luxurious armchair.

Media Guy apologizes to cameraman: "I am sorry... Awfully sorry. Traffic jam, you know. Hmmm..."

Finally, he sits in his special anchor armchair, close to Minister, at 3 to 4 feet distance and starts interview.

Chapter 11

Now, everything is okay. Media Guy, acts as experienced journalist, begins interviewing British Minister of Health, rather tall, slim blond-red hair man, almost typical British.

Media Guy looks at camera: "Hello, Ladies and Gentlemen this is USFTV. Sorry we are little bit late... Hmm, 90 seconds... Never mind 90 seconds versus 90 years of human being life... Let's go to the point. Today we are honored to talk with the first man of British health... Mr. Peter Atkins."

British minister of health delivers official smile as each politician and greets audience: "Hello... First, good luck to American people... And good health, of course... I, really, do hope this interview will be useful and interesting both for ordinary people and health professionals...

Media Guy approving Minister's statement talks to camera: "Yeah... I agree with you completely. We are supposed to answer questions of USFTV spectators. The first is... Will be some fatal diseases like cancer or aids rooted out in 21st century?"

British minister of health makes serious and worried face: "Oh, Jesus, so hard question at the very beginning. What could I expect at the end? Never mind, all right. Unfortunately, I'm not quite sure that answer could be positive. Nowadays, we have simultaneous process of virus mutations with scientists' efforts to discover medicine for cancer and aids…Aids and cancer will be curable, but we shall face new diseases, as well."

Media Guy continues his interview: "Yeah… But… What do you mean about youth education. I mean on avoiding risky way of life". He suddenly starts gesticulating. "Like… Smoking, narcotics, alcoholic drinks and unsafe sex…"

British minister of health answers: "Hmm, good question. Role of education institutions is very important… But I'm not in charge of that field… You'd better ask Minister of Education."

Media Guy sees he asked wrong person: "Sorry, You are right… That's education issue." At that point hostess, young beautiful blonde girl appears wearing very short skirt. She brings with her small pile of papers with questions of TV spectators. Both Media Guy and Minister are starring at her as if they are hypnotized. Seeing beautiful girl Media Guy remembers his voyeur experience. Of course, he is in studio on air. He and his minds are absent, present in studio in pure physical sense.

He remembers him as 10-years old kid with nose stuck to the window of ladies locker room. Five young girls are undressing underwear staying totally nude for a while. Girls' giggling is heard in locker room. Very young Media Guy was hypnotized face pressed against small window of the basement ladies' locker room. That was his first visual experience with woman naked body, tits with nipples on the top and small bushes on their privy parts.

Media Guy as if suddenly awakes up from deep sleep. Short dream that was his childhood experience is definitely over. He immediately makes out he's on air and starts searching pile of question papers located on a small glass table in front of him and Minister.

"Yeah", looks at one paper. "Oh, no... No this". He is taking another and looks at it. "Oh, Jesus... This one is not appropriate too. Just a second. I guess this one is real American... wise and serious question."

British minister of health says, snapping fingers: "I hope so..."

Media Guy finally cheerful starts loud reading of question: "Hey... Cocksuckers... What craps are you talking about? Aids". He is smiling to Minister as apology for reading wrong letter. "Hmm... That is American free style... You know, America is free country, so sometimes, people exaggerate using colloquial terms".

British minister of health makes wide cynical smile: "Well, I see...People usually takes freedom as granted in wrong way. Just keep on reading ". He bursts in laughter.

Media Guy tries to hide he is very confused; continues reading questions loudly:

"I want to fuck... Fuck blondes... Fuck brunettes... Fuck redheads..."

Media Guy repeated mistake, his face turned pale, he starts apologizing again: Oh, my Lord. What's this. I'm awfully sorry.

British minister of health smiles: "Of course, this could be only American style...We, British are more traditional, maybe too conservative. For sure, this could be seen only on American networks."

Media Guy feels ashamed, first time in front of camera, however keeps on reading: "Aids doesn't matter me... I didn't cut off my cock... And you... You are doing it literally by all those craps about safe sex... What am I supposed to do?!? To buy a rubber doll in sex shop... Fuck all the theories... We do have only one life...What's the life without sex... My message is... Let's spend fucking each single minute of our damned, only life..."

At that point young hostess appears holding small tray with two narrow long glasses of lemon juice. She puts glasses on a small glass table, then leaves the studio. Seeing again beautiful girl Media Guy returns to his childhood voyeur experience forgetting he's in studio interviewing British minister of health. He looks absentminded but happy.

Five nude, young girls are taking shower. Sight is vague due to heavy steam in shower room. So girls nudity is soft – not a single close shot of girls asses or hairy pubises. Girls' loud giggling follows taking shower. Kid's face is pressed against small window of the basement ladies shower room.

Media Guy suddenly awakes from the state of hypnosis. He says: "Yeah... This is too free... Let's go to some more serious question. This, for instance." Media Guy takes small piece of paper starting reading: "I am college girl afraid of aids... But I like group sex... Uhh..." His face suddenly blushes, feels ashamed. "Sorry, I am awfully sorry Minister and audience in front of TV", Media Guy apologizes.

British minister of health smiling; tries to make Media Guy not to feel uncomfortable: "Never mind... I understand problems of modern youngsters... Maybe we, British are little bit more conservative than we should be..."

At that point Media Guy starts intensive scratching his arms and his beck. That's probably some bug. At very first time British minister is shocked by strange behavior of Media Guy in front of camera. But suddenly minister joined to Media Guy by scratching his head, arms, beck and legs. Now, both of them perform highly intensive body scratching losing control upon their behavior and forgetting they are in front of camera. It looks really funny.

Obviously, bugs make great troubles. Losing control of situation due to intensive scratching Media Guy pushes the long glass of lemon juice, which is split over upper part of minister's trousers. Now, it looks as if Minister is pissed. Media Guy is close to state of shock terribly afraid of possible upcoming consequences. Minister is shocked too.

Media Guy, lost minded, kneels on his knees in front of Minister trying to correct the horrible mistake. His head is close to upper part of Minister's trousers and his hands on Minister's thighs.

British minister of health extremely shocked, putting hands on head exclaiming:
"Oh, God! What kind of people, for the Christ sake, you Americans are?"

Chapter 12

Office of Editor in Chief; atmosphere is extremely overstrained due to scandalous interview with British minister of health. Editor in Chief, furious walks around the office aimlessly. Media Guy, silent and confused feels something bad will happen.

Editor in Chief in very loud voice speaks insulting words to Media Guy:
"Jesus! What idiot you are! Tell me how it happened?" He still keeps aimless walking through the office trying to reduce anger.
"Me... and... USFTV are ashamed... ashamed as never so far. What for? What for?
For the sake... Oh, my God...for the sake of an complete idiot!", he says, putting hands on his head.

Media Guy is unusually silent, makes out he made terrible mistake. He realizes the best is, at that point, not to speak any word.

Editor in Chief still furious: "You... You... Hmm... Not to mention possible international problem! You, bastard... It's likely you corrupted political relations between US and United Kingdom"
Media Guy To asks in shy fearful voice: "Wh... What international problem? What political relations has to do with spilt juice. I really don't understand"

Editor in Chief looks slightly less furious tries to explain Media Guy: "Between U.S. and Great Britain... and... You know what... Hmm, next step could be bankruptcy of this electronic media...What crook you are." He makes unusual grimaces, starts sobbing: "Damn me... Damn the day I hired you... Bastard!"

He comes very close to Media Guy looking straight forward to his eyes very angry: "Not you! That's me who is an idiot! Why! Do you know why!?! Yes... I hired you... That's why I am the greatest idiot on the face of the planet Earth."

Media Guy is very confused and sad about this: "So what... What can I do to correct this what happened?"

Editor in Chief cannot answer any question to person like Media Guy, person that cannot understand anything. He cries angrily: "So what... So what...That's only what you can say... Oh shit... That's unbelievable... What kind of man you are... Not to mention you as journalist... Professional... Hmm it looks as if it doesn't bother you... Unbelievable!"

Media Guy crashed, ashamed, humble in bad mood, silent: "Yeah... I see... That mistake is real disaster... Hmm... What fool I am... Spilt juice on minister's trousers... Horrible... I do hope that won't cause war between America and Britain".

Editor in Chief's face is very worried: "Yeah... Spilt juice on minister's trousers in this case is political issue... Not any casual accident...You must know it as journalist."

Media Guy in sarcastic voice: "Oh, really... What is that crucial I should know! Maybe those trousers on Minister are Foreign Affairs matter... Oh, Jesus help me... It has just happened...It has just happened as simple as that...

Can't you make out what I'm talking about... Dear boss...?"

Editor in Chief furious over such comments, very loud to Media Guy pointing at entrance door: "Now it's enough! I am fed up of you! GET LOST OF HERE!

GET LOST OF USFTV! And please, do not call me ever, ever again... YOU ARE FIRED! And... Listen to me carefully...I don't want to hear even the first letter of your name, ever!!!"

Media Guy is leaving the office slamming the door. He figures out that could be the end of his media career. His long live optimism has lost in an conversation with boss.

Chapter 13

Media Guy is terribly shocked. For the first time in his life he is fired. He has been a step from firing many times during his media career, but now he is fired for real. Aimless roaming through the streets becomes part of his life.

Nice evening, clear sky, shopping area in downtown street. Media Guy stops in front of luxurious window shop, where rather expensive HI-TECH gadgets are displayed – computers, TV and audio etc… Having in mind his position of unemployed person he stares at price tags sadly. He knows that job loss is loss of money and personal integrity. Nobody wants unemployed friends, even cousins.

Media Guy talks to himself: "Yeah… From now on… I am only eccentric voyeur not customer… Hmm… I guess being unemployed is some kind of perversion here in U.S.A."

Leaving window of HI-TECH shop Media Guy continues walking. Late evening hours, a very few people in the streets. Even outside street atmosphere is not cheerful. After a short walk he stops again; at this point in front of Chrysler automobile showroom.

Media Guy is looking at cars displayed; speaks to himself: "Oh, oh my God tell me… Please tell me whether I'll ever be the owner of one of these nice brand new cars… Hmm… Shit… What tragedy to be unemployed… No credit records… No loans… No mortgage… No leasing… Finally, in one word no life at all!"

Shortly after figuring out that it's more fantasy Media Guy leaves Chrysler automobile showroom keeping his walk through downtown streets. It's free for now. But it's part of human being psychology – to look at merchandise he or she cannot afford. And once more he stops in front of window of Ladies Fashion Shop.

Media Guy surprised puts hands on his head: "Oh yeah…I forgot to mention… Girls." He is making sad but funny faces in his "psychological sufferings"

"No life…no job… no girls… how tragic my life is… Shit… Susan loves me… I really do hope… But who will marry me…unemployed person who cannot afford anything. For sure, she is a smart girl she will find another guy," Media Guy says.

While looking at expensive brand name ladies clothes in window he continues talking to himself: "There is nothing I could buy her for present… I'd better leave this place otherwise I'll must call ambulance."

He continues walking without turning to fully illuminated shop windows. Trying to forget and to reduce his troubles Media Guy starts whistling. *Stop thinking on job loss is the only efficient medicament*, Media Guy thinks.

Chapter 14

Waiting room in Welfare office crowded with people who are on social assistance. They are mostly minorities – black people as well as people from South America and Eastern Europe. Majorities of people are sitting aimlessly looking at nothing. That's typical for unemployed in U.S.A. – the only thing they have is hope that must destroy dangerous apathy. They all wait to be interviewed by welfare social worker. They got numbers and listen to loudspeaker to hear numbers which means they should enter social worker office for interview.

Media Guy has number 44. He is sitting between one big black man and one big and fat Mexican man. All three have glass look as if they are narcotized. Big black man has a chewing gum in mouth while fat big Mexican and Media Guy eat some crackers pulling out piece by piece from small colored bags. All three seem to be nervous and look funny. Mexican guy has black moustaches and vivid sombrero on his head while black guy has a small cap.

Voice from one loudspeaker: "Number 44!"

Media Guy figuring out it's his turn tries to get rid of small colored bag of crackers. First he offers it to Black guy. Seeing Black guy strange mute face he offers it to Mexican. Unfortunately, there is no response again. Media Guy confronts himself with strange, stoned face again.

"Number 44! Number 44," voice from loudspeaker again.

Seeing he hasn't much time Media Guy throws it in trash basket. Then he leaves waiting room hurrying up for interview.

Chapter 15

Welfare office. Social worker, mid-aged woman looks at filled application form for social assistance. Media Guy is sitting impatiently across from social worker.

Social worker is looking at application form line by line; talks to herself: "Okay... Okay... Good..." She keeps thorough checking of application form fields: "Fine... Sex... Male... Very good... Birth date. Well."

Media Guy as if he speaks to himself, very silent: "Male, for sure... No doubt about that... You can check it"
Social worker hearing his statement a bit surprised she shifts her look from application form to Media Guy: "I beg you pardon, gentleman?"
Media Guy figures out he is supposed to answer the questions not to deliver statements, in particular stupid ones: "I am sorry...So sorry dear lady."
Social worker in very official cold voice: "Oh no... Never mind... Please, don't apologize."
She is focusing her look at application form again and continues checking the form line by line, word by word. All entered data must be perfectly correct.

Media Guy gets very impatient, nervous trying to sit calm. But no use, he makes some funny and strange faces fidgeting and looking social worker in the face as if he is in charge of checking application form, not she. Situation becomes strange.

Social worker now surprised delivers a short reproachful glance at Media Guy:

"Pardon... Just a moment" She checks again application form and says: "Oh, yeah... You are journalist... And... Sorry, You have been journalist... And... Not of whatsoever kind... You have been employed with an electronic media... TV company"

Media Guy confirms: "Yes... You are right... But now it's past... At this point I am unemployed."

Social worker as if she doesn't hear him talks her story: "Yeah...Many of our cases are not understood geniuses... Writers, actors, painters...Hmmm, journalists... Et cetera... Creative, but unemployed people."

Media Guy don't like this way of comfort words, nervous: "So what... I guess it has nothing to do with me... Let's put aside philosophy."

Social worker continues her statement: "Maybe... But when people choose some real profession as business, programming, technical jobs usually are employed almost all time... guys can't you understand, no use living on fantasies... Do you happen to know, for instance, I was the best singer in High School chorus."

Media Guy finally figures out that this is not any accordance with aim of his visit to Welfare Office. However, he tries to comfort her: "I see... You have outstanding voice... Great talent. Probably here due to lack of marketing support".

Social worker sad with nostalgia: "Yeah... And Today I am an office rat filing these stupid forms. I must interview people whose feet are not on ground... Like you... Can you imagine it?"

Media Guy gets a bit angry since he is not here to waste his time: "Hey, hey why me!?! What about my social assistance."

Social worker getting involved deeply in remembers and past experience with nostalgia: "Oh, I forgot to tell you I was Miss in my birthplace and I was on cover pages in local newspapers." She starts sobbing

Media Guy is mocking her but tries to be official: "Well... Singing talent... Then extraordinary beauty... Why are you here in this rotten Welfare office?"

Social worker explains: "Yeahh... Way of life of show business people is unacceptable for me... You know it better than me... Editors, even photographers blackmailed girls asking them to have sex."

Media Guy in cold voice as if it's unusual: "Yeah... I see... disgusting... So what, is it, really, so awful?!? To have sex."

Social worker at that point gets annoyed with his statement: "Yeah... You crook... You are Media Guy... You are the same bastard as they!!!

She is obviously nervous, starts trembling and crying losing control over herself.

Chapter 16

Having no money Media Guy was enforced to work various, mainly unskilled jobs to afford living. More precisely those temporary jobs are more like troubles than decent profession for him. Pizza delivery was first his job of such kind.

Media Guy drives Pizza delivery vehicle, ordinary car. Back seats are overloaded with packages of ordered pizzas. There is music in pizza delivery car. He is searching for exact address by turning head left and right alternately. At the same time he is humming some pleasant song.

Media Guy happy about finally seeing wanted number-address: "Whaa… Finally I've got here. This is a big order. Yeahh… 50 pizzas… Must be a great party"

He is looking at the house while sitting in delivery vehicle: "Let's go… to deliver pizzas."

Media Guy is opening rear doors. He tries to take all 50 packages in his arms. It seems pretty difficult. Pizzas piling process looks extraordinary problematic and when Media Guy is doing it very funny too. Half of Media Guy is inside car trying to take packages from rear seats. Another half or even less at some points is outside car.

Media Guy gets suddenly very nervous: "Shit… Hmm…"

Finally he succeeds in taking all 50 pizzas in his arms. Now packages are more than a half of his height. He starts moaning, but happy.

"Yooppiee! Let's go taking tip," he says to himself.

Shortly after leaving delivery vehicle Media Guy trips falling down on a driveway to the house. All packages are scattered and many pizzas are outside packages.

Chapter 17
Telemarketing job

Telemarketing department; Media Guy with earphones and microphone set on his head sitting in his box illuminated by neon lights. Atmosphere in telemarketing department is very busy. It's noisy due to many telemarketing persons interviewing over phones.

Media Guy: "Good evening, we'll ask you couple of questions. This is poll."

Person 1 over phone loud: "What idiot you are! I watch my favorite series… Go to the Hell!!!" He is slamming the receiver.

Media Guy: "Hello, young lady… Telemarketing department… I need just couple of answers. It will last very short, believe me very short."

Lady furious over phone: "Fuck yourself, jerk… You interrupted me making love with my lover in bathroom… Bastard!" She is slamming receiver.

Media Guy no matter what's going on regarding his telemarketing persons he still remains self-confident: "Nice evening, isn't it… First question – What was your income for the last year? Hmm…"

Person 2 furious over phone: "Mm... My... Income! It has nothing to do with your business, jerk! Listen to me, carefully. FUCK OFF IDIOT!" He is slamming receiver.

Media Guy as real professional telemarketing agent continues as if everything is okay: "Hello... Mister, how old are you? Please let us know... That's only a short poll... Won't last long, couple of minutes."

Person 2 over phone: "I am... Okay, I'll tell you... wait a moment..."
Rather loud sound of ass activity is heard, It is sound of human parting.
Person 2 is bursting in laughter over phone.

"Now, you know my age. I was quite clear... Ha, ha, ha. Have you some other questions? Just ask," Person 2 says.

Media Guy is now shocked: "That's not fair... Really, it has nothing to do with good manners... That's disgusting. I feel sick!"

He is slamming the receiver, takes off headphone set throwing it on the floor.

Chapter 18
Factory worker

Big factory; engine room. All engines work at full capacity. Engines make big noise so workers can't talk to each other. There are several moving production lines. Media Guy is next to one of them – an unending production line. He is wearing blue worker's uniform with some funny cap on his head. On his left side is another worker – fat mid-aged man. In the case of Media Guy missing to pick up product from line another worker must do it. That job is very dull and quite mechanical; therefore Media Guy is not happy about that. Not any knowledge or talent is required. Those workers look like real robots.

Media Guy is doing stupid programmed manual motions of picking up items and putting them in box located about three feet from unending production line.

He tries to tell something to another worker who is close to him: "Hey! Hey! Hey, man! I must go to toilet."

Worker doesn't hear him well: "Pardon! What! I don't hear you! What did you tell?"

Media Guy is nervous, taking another worker's head directly to ear extremely loud: "I do have to go in toilet! In other words... I must go pissing!!! Pissing."

Workers replies calm: "So what!?! We all sometimes piss, not only you. Can't you wait for half an hour... We have lunch break... Why are you so impatient?
Hmm... You are like primary school kid."

Media Guy gets angry: "Yeah... Thanks a lot... Shit... Now it's late."

He pissed in his uniform, lower part is obviously wet, dark circle is seen. Media Guy felt embarrassed.

Chapter 19
Stripping job

Striptease club for ladies. Several male strippers are dancing erotic dance on the stage. Rich light show is on; loud disco music is heard. Ladies are in laughter having fun looking at nude males. Only dancer wear is slips – panties that cover only genitals. Some women try to make a kind of private extra show by putting banknotes in strippers' panties. Atmosphere is very cheerful. Same Striptease club for ladies but empty. Actually, not quite empty. There is a jury of three ladies in 30's – blonde, redhead and brunette. Their task is to evaluate male strippers for hiring. For sure not all strippers have a chance to be hired. That is Stripping audition.

Three nice cheerful ladies are chatting. They sit about 10 feet from the stripping stage drinking some cocktails eager to see young nude males. It's on them to make final decision on hiring. Among many males looking for stripping job is Media Guy too. They wait for their turn in locker room. Some of them are in jeans, some in suits but all very nervous and eager to get stripping job. Audition is starting. First male is throwing piece by piece his clothing trying to follow the rhythm of loud music dancing erotically. Three ladies star at him. Finally he is totally nude. Ladies are happy about that.

Three ladies are loud sighing at same time looking at nude male: "Oh… This male is really good! Hired!"

"Look at this…What legs…ass…balls, long penis. Oh, sorry, we got rude." they apologize to each other, then burst in laughter.

Another male is stripping dancing erotically. Light show and music follow his stripping moves. Another male totally nude in front of female wide open eyes.

Three ladies again in one voice; obviously not satisfied with male on the stage: "Okay, that's enough… You can go home. Better luck next time Another one, please!"

Male stripper on stage protests: "Hey, hey, beauties! I didn't finished. I've just started… Let me finish stripping masterpiece…" He is in trousers and shirt without sleeves.

Three ladies at the same time as one ironically: "Hey, Honey! That's okay… You are free to go gome… Please, leave the stage immediately.Another! Please!"

Media Guy is another stripper. He starts dancing and stripping. Fortunately or maybe, unfortunately, doing it very, very clumsy and funny. Three ladies laugh at him wondering how he could even imagine being stripper. He got more confused seeing ladies in intensive laughter. Ladies forgot to stop him stripping enjoying funny piece. Finally, Media Guy got angry about that so he has thrown last piece – his panties exactly on their glasses with cocktails. Cocktails splash faces of three ladies. Ladies are shocked pulling out handkerchieves from his bags start cleaning drops of cocktail from their faces. Ladies look strange and funny with make up smeared up all over their faces. Seeing them Media Guy bursts in laughter.

Chapter 20

Due to his unemployment Media Guy moved to very small apartment in the lower rated city area. He is sitting in armchair with legs on small table in front of him and watching TV. In his right hand is remote control in left can of beer. While changing TV channels Media Guy eats some crackers and drinks beer.

He is very nervous and cause is not TV program as it looks at first glance but probably his status of unemployed person.

Media Guy nervous clicking remote control button for changing TV channels:

"Shit! What craps they broadcasted, do they mean we are idiots!"

Media Guy is talking to himself loud, chewing crackers: "Yeah… More than 100 channels… and nothing worth seeing… Hmm…that's America today.

Craps… No jobs but TV channels… As much as you like."

He keeps on changing TV channels as well as eating crackers and drinking can of beer: "Yeah… TV critics and psychologists are quite right… All you can see is violence, sex, drugs and perversion… Yeah, that's all". His speech is followed by very deep sigh of great disappointment.

"Soccer… That's better", cries Media Guy cheerfully. After a couple of seconds Media Guy gets disappointed again: "Oh, no… third class teams… What for I pay cable fee? For this broadcasted bullshit."

He is putting a can of beer on small table next to him and with left hand free starts intensive picking nose. Busy with changing TV channels and picking nose Media Guy stops using remote control after getting USFTV on screen

Media Guy surprised seeing his former company and Editor in Chief speaks: "Oh... What's this! Oh, Jesus... Look at him... Media Star... Pardon Mega Star. Big Editor in Chief... Source of Wisdom." He is very sarcastic imitating Editor in Chief speaking. Media Guy makes funny faces and mouth as if he has a hot potato inside.

"Bastard!!! How dare you speak, son of bitch!!! You, that you who fired me. And ruined my whole life. Crook", says Media Guy getting furious, losing control over himself throws remote control aiming at Editor in Chief on TV screen.

Chapter 21

Welfare office; Media Guy is sitting across social worker, mid-aged woman with thick glasses. He fidgets nervously and chews chewing gum extremely intensively as if he ruminates like a cow. Social worker is reading some papers with her nose stuck into files.

Social worker makes detailed looking at files. To Media Guy: "Well... How is your searching for job?"

Media Guy as if he didn't hear the question: "I beg you pardon lady?"

Social worker continues: "Okay. Do you, mister... perform intensive looking for job?" She is raising her head and looking straightforward at Media Guy eyes: "Am I clear now? I guess, Yes."

Media Guy keeps on ruminating: "Oh, yes...Of course. I do my best to find some job...Lady!" I speak the true and nothing more and less than bare true."

Social worker obviously not impressed by his statement: "Yeah... I see... But... No results so far... Am I right."

Media Guy is getting very nervous, still ruminating: "You say no results... Hmm... no results... So what can I do... Not enough jobs... That's free market economy, dear lady... Can't you understand it!?! Free market sometimes means be free of job".

Social worker in serious voice: "Okay, let's put philosophy aside and get straightforward to the point. You cannot be on welfare forever."

Media Guy starring at social worker sarcastic: "Oh, really… I don't know. Well. Help me."

Social Worker not happy by such behavior of social assistance applicant says in warning voice: "You must find some job… any job… It's not necessary to be employed with media. There are many other jobs, maybe not so attractive as in media. But, we cannot make happy all applicants."

Media Guy gets angry, stands up looking at her face: "You… Lady… What, for the Christ sake, do you want me to do? Maybe, being manual unskilled worker! Hey, dear lady I was journalist employed with electronic media. Is that clear?"

Social worker tries to calm him: "Hey, hey… take it easy…yeah. The fact is that you were employed! But now you are unemployed and on social assistance… that's, unfortunately the truth… The whole pure truth."

Chapter 22

Small but nice downtown cafeteria not crowded but not empty too. It's rather noisy. Media Guy and his girl Susan sit next to cafeteria window glancing at each other interrupting it by looking at the street through cafeteria window. They are mute not talking to each other. Atmosphere is unpleasant – tense situation.

Media Guy is getting bored with silence of his beloved girl: "Well… I really do hope you still have tongue. So you can speak something. Whatever you want. But speak something."

Girl: "Okay… Do you have something to say?!? You can speak too."

Media Guy in nervous voice: "To speak… what to speak? What do you mean?!? You are the person who called me this morning and said, quotation: *"I must see you. I do have something very important to tell you…"* So, I am waiting for your historical words… Just do what you have to do… Speak what you have in your mind."

Girl is hesitating as if she is not willing to say what she really wanted to say: "You are nice man…well brought-up… But… But".

Media Guy is getting more and more nervous, speaks so loudly that some visitors in cafeteria pay attention by looking at Media Guy table: "But…but… what about but… Hmm… Please, go straight to the point."

Girl keeps talking, shy, hesitates; she cannot look at eyes of Media Guy, feels unpleasant for attracting attention of cafeteria visitors: "You know… Hmm. You are on welfare…"

Media Guy really angry, very loud: "So what!!! What am I supposed to do? Maybe, to commit suicide… It could be the best option for U.S. taxpayers… Oh, no… no, no and definitely no! However I'll find another job."

Girl sharply replies: "Then great… Just go ahead. Find a job."

Waitress, young blonde girl asks them for order, wide smiling: "Would you like something to drink?"

Media Guy sharply replies as thunder ball strike: "Ice coffee… An ice coffee for me." He asks his girl: "What is your will, Honey?"

Girl replies after several seconds: "Maybe… Hmm… Ice coffee too."

Waitress in very pleasant voice: "Okay… Two glasses of ice coffee". She is leaving their table to bring ordered drinks.

Girl continues speaking: "Unfortunately, I must tell you that." Her voice is trembling. "I don't want to share my life… my only life with man on social assistance," she says feeling bad.

Media Guy, starring at her, pretends as if he listening to her extremely carefully.

Girl continues: "I need as every woman… support. It's not usual that woman supports man, particular in financial field… Yeah… That's it".

At that point she feels slightly better for she has just said what she had in her brain and her heart. Break up. that was something inevitable in such occasions.

Waitress is approaching to their table with thin nice smile on her mouth: "Here is your order." She is putting glasses of ice coffee on table. Her very short skirt enables seeing beautiful legs. Media Guy with head close to her looks at her legs as if he is hypnotized.

"Well, enjoy ice coffee", waitress says leaving their table. Media Guy turns his head towards her long legs as if he is still hypnotized.

Girl seeing he doesn't listen to her, speaks louder: "Hey, hey man! I am talking to you! I announce that at this point I am breaking off with you! Do you hear me!"

Media Guy as if his hypnosis suddenly stops: "What! What do you say. I don't care! Go... Just go wherever your heart like! I don't give a shit"

He continues in provocative way: "Your ass... Your tits...and frankly... legs are really horrible... third class comparing to hers. Just look at the legs of this waitress."

Media Guy is showing her pointing a finger at waitress.

Girl is furious now, starts crying: "Wh... Wha... What! I am not beautiful! Fuck yourself, bastard!!! I was Miss in High School. Who, do you think you are, idiot!"

She takes her glass of ice coffee pouring it over himself and goes towards exit door.

Chapter 23

Media Guy makes a dinner in small apartment. He is cheerful as if his girl didn't break off with him. He even whistles some pleasant well-known melody making fruit cocktail in an electronic mixer. Then he pours cocktail in oval glass.

Media Guy is drinking toast to himself. Solo drinker, alone without girl who left him searching for a man who can provide better future to her.

Media Guy: "To my health... God bless me... Long-live me... Lucky me. Now, all ladies on the face of the world are accessible. I am single player." He is preparing substance for pancakes – it seems he is very committed to that activity whistling all time.

Media Guy talks to himself still obsessed by former girl: "She... She was Miss in High School... Hmm... Ridiculous... Yeah... And I was I was Mister of City Beach."

He is bursting in laughter for a while: "Oh, no...No, that's me who is complete fool... Not her... Yeah, she has been with me due to my job not due to honest true love... My sweet... My former Honey... wanted to boast off my profession... Hmm, shit – electronic media journalist – star... Oh, never mind... just forget her... Go further... This planet is full of nice girls."

Media Guy starts pouring pancake substance in a big frying pan and making pancakes. While whistling he turns another pancake side by throwing it in the air and catching using gravitational force. Although he does his best it looks clumsy and funny. That's likely for break off with Susan.

Media Guy is throwing pancake high in the air: "Oh, oh, oh... Yuppie! I catch you, bloody pancake!"

Media Guy pancake making moves are more like modern dancing than cooking. Very amusing performance theatre. Interrupted by sudden loud phone ringing he missed to catch another pancake and instead to be in pan it fell on his head covering all face. Thanks to small size of apartment, he hire due to lack of money, he shortly finds telephone handset.

Media Guy still covered face with pancake takes receiver: "Who is this. Yes... Oh, yes!"

Editor in Chief over phone, sounds very polite: "You are again with us... Member of USFTV...Please, come tomorrow to my office... There are lot of business that must be done."

Media Guy happy and shocked by this phone call at same time: "Wh. Wh. Wha... What!!! I am hired... Great!" He acts as if it's something unbelieveable.

Editor in Chief over phone: "Yes! Yes, you are hired, again! Sorry, for I have done to you, but you made great bullshit."

Media Guy makes loud happy exclamation: "Yooppiieee!" He removes pancake from his face kissing and cheerfully throwing it at TV.

Chapter 24

Media Guy is entering USFTV Headquarters. Security guard at reception desk looks happy about seeing him again.

Security guard very cheerful, loudly: "Hey, hey! Media Guy... Friend of mine! Where are you?!? I haven't see for ages. Again with us! I hope... Am I right?"

Media Guy replies waving right hand with wide ear to ear smile: "I guess yes! Maybe... Who knows!" He stops in front of elevator impatiently waiting.

Editor in Chief office, Media Guy is sitting in leather luxurious armchair while Editor in Chief is walking nervously through the office. From time to time he stops next to big window starring aimlessly outside.

Editor in chief as if he apologizes, act as person who feels guilt to Media Guy:

"I am sorry... But... You made lot of troubles to our company... USFTV has been forced to pay fine as compensation to British Minister and British Government... Yeah... His reputation is offended... Hmm... Craps, on one hand... but on the other hand it could be some kind of advertising... Hmm, could be... That's strange attraction of ambiguity of media and journalism at all."

Media Guy figures out how complex, hard and unpredictable journalism job is.

He is nodding to him: "Yes... You are right."

Editor in Chief continues: "But it's past... Forget it... You are again with USFTV crew... Hmm... And I must say one of our Top Guns... Frankly, your performance oscillates from extraordinary to terrible... You can increase our rating to the top, and decrease to the very bottom level within just an hour. That's shocking and fascinating at same time."

Media Guy is happy by such words approves it: "Yeah. Top Gun. I agree."

Editor in Chief mobile phone is ringing. He takes phone pulling it out from inside pocket of his suit.

Editor in Chief starts talking over mobile phone: "Yes... Yes... I see... Okay... Yeah... Just a moment."

He takes pencil and small piece of paper: "How did you say? Yes, I see." He is writing some address on small piece of paper.

"Okay... Yes... I know... Bye, bye," Editor in Chief says finishing talking over mobile phone. He returns mobile phone in his jacket pocket.

Editor in Chief looks confused and anxious: "Some lunatic is trying to commit suicide by jumping from high building... I guess assignment is exactly for you... here is the address." He delivers small piece of paper with location address to Media Guy.

"It's not far from here... Just hurry up! Good Luck Media Guy", Editor in Chief says with easy smile on his face.

Media Guy in rush leaving the office, loudly to Editor: "Don't worry, I promise you I'll do my best!"

Chapter 25

Media Guy gets out of elevator rushing towards Suicide person who stands on the very edge of the building. Due to preventing commitment of suicide Media Guy sharply warns cameraman to stay invisible for Suicide person.

Media Guy to cameraman very loudly: "Hey, hey! No chance!!! Your position must be invisible to him... Other-wise we must take partial responsibility if he jumps... Is that clear!"

Cameraman replies not used to see Media Guy behaves that way; almost afraid replies: "Oh, yes... Sure, I see... Take it's done."

Media Guy approaches some 10 to 15 feet to Suicide person who stands on cornice. It's rather high – approximately 200 feet. Crowd of people gathers on the street to see the "show" – the outcome of struggle for life.

Crowd on the street focus their eyes to Suicide person showing worried and scared faces eager to know the solution to this sensitive issue. Most of them are mute some comment on the situation. At that point Suicide person notices Media Guy.

Suicide person, slim dark hair male about 30 years, shocked, frenzied to Media Guy: "Oh, Jeuss, no... No, no, no... Who, the hell, are you, now?!? Tell the truth."

Media Guy pretends as if hie is not confused, trying to make suicide person calm and safe; gentle: "Friend of yours... Believe me. True friend."

Suicide person not sure about him still frenzied as if he has some mental attack: "Really. That's sounds heart-breaking... You. You friend of mine. I have not any friend, bastard!"

Media Guy still remains calm almost invisibly approaching to suicide person – inch by inch: "Yes, I am... your truly friend...Believe me... Why don't you believe me?"

Media Guy does his best to hide his own fear; but no use his lips are trembling and drops of sweat are visible on his face. From this point on he considers himself as savior, not journalist. From now on his assignment is to save this guy who can kill himself within seconds. Good report is not primary task, but saving one young life. By doing it he will become local, maybe national hero. That is something that must be everybody be proud of.

Seeing Media Guy comes closer to him Suicide person cries: "Ohh. Noo. No. Stay where you are... I order stay where you are... I warn you without the slightest motion... Or..." He moves couple of inches closer to air staying on cornice. It seems a step closer to sure death.

Media Guy is really frightened. He is absolutely sure he doesn't want to report, but to prevent death. He cries: "No! No! Do not do it! Please, listen to your friend"

Suicide person frenzied keeps his style of commu-nication to Media Guy: "Oh, yes. You'll tell me! Hmm, you are not my friend. I, even, don't know who you are. I see your perverted eyes... You must be TV journalist. Who other could be?!?"

Media Guy still frightened about outcome of this assignment, try to be more convincing: "Once again... I am your friend for real... I am here to help you...otherwise I shouldn't be here... Believe me!"

Suicide person even more frenzied and sarcastic to Media Guy: "Oh, really... My dollar friend comes to me to cash my death... Hmm, where is photograph, cameraman... Oh, yeah... How stupid I am...They are on the ground to make the best shots of my dead body... I see, Live coverage of death, That's the only thing you want from me".

Media Guy denies it but he is not convinced too: "No, you are not right at all... I am here just for one reason. To help you... Do you hear – To help you! Your life matters not report or live coverage."

Suicide person cannot believe Media Guy, ironically: "Wh... What! To help me! You journalists to help? To whom you can help, by your lies". Suicide person bursts in laughter.

"You are here just for one reason - to get extra money...Higher bonus for shooting me dead or alive... Better dead...Both is the best... It's nothing more or less than pure self-promotion. That's why are you here... Does it make sense? Of course, it's all about money... In this fucking modern society only money makes the sense!" Suicide person says.

At that point sound of sirens is heard. Several vehicles – Fire dept. Police and ambulance stop next to building. Seeing it rush Suicide person steps into open air to jump from building. As never so far Media Guy does something as if he is James Bond 007. Like a tiger Media Guy makes a sudden long jump succeeding to catch Suicide person. At that point very loud sigh of uncertainty and fear is heard – "OOOHHH"...

Now both of them – Media Guy and Suicide person hang in the air holding firmly edge of cornice with their hands. Fortunately, Fire dept. Rescue Squad puts within seconds special air filled mattress for saving. At that point of Media Guy's catching Suicide person something unusual has happened.

Suicide person panic-stricken seeing what he has done caught Media Guy trousers and took it off. So Media Guy stayed in underwear – in panties that looks funny – white color with pink flowers and violet butterflies. It looks like Gay underwear fashion design.

Now, Media Guy trousers are hung on his shoes, so everybody in the crowd can see his legs and panties. His bare legs are not so impressive. However, they are enough far away from ladies and other persons eyes on the street for detailed analysis. Moment of making Media Guy legs and panties visible causes Ladies' deep sigh of sudden passion. Some ladies even pull out small binoculars from their bags to see better great view – Media Guy nude legs and interesting panties.

Upon seeing saving mattress below them Suicide person and Media Guy open their clenched fists to fall on mattress. Both of them are saved but accident has happened.

After falling Suicide person suddenly pumps air out of mattress. Media Guy falling was couple of seconds later – enough to be hurt, fortunately not bad.
Crowd exclamation of relief is heard.

Chapter 26

Doctors decided to hospitalize Media Guy for several days. He was hurt while he was saving life of Suicide person. Media Guy has some big bruises and scratches on his face and arms. He feels pains in his whole body. Don't matter pains Media Guy has become the hero in the eyes of people.

Media Guy lies in hospital bed. Suicide person with his parents and two sisters approach to Media Guy bed. All his family wants to thank Media Guy for saving life. Family of five makes a line on the right side of his bed. Media Guy is not happy to see them but pretends as if he is leering at them.

Suicide person tapping Media Guy on right shoulder: "There are no words…I can…express gratitude to you… Great man with great heart." After that he starts weeping.

Media Guy at the point of tapping his shoulder makes painful exclamation: "Ooouchhh! My poor shoulder…". His face is almost distorted due to grimace.

Suicide person introducing members of his family to Media Guy, pointing at his sisters: "These ladies are my sisters, Hero… My savior".

Two sisters cheerful in one voice with thin smiles, happy to see hero for the first time in their life: "Yes… Hero… Oh… We must get the autograph from you… Oh, Hero you must give us your autograph." They act as if they are teenage girls, thrilled to see hero in reality.

Suicide person sharply to his sisters: "Maybe later. Now you have to be patien." He points at an old man approaching Media Guy hospital bed: "Hmm. Now, this man with gray hair is my father."

Media Guy doesn't want visitors to see he is disturbed. All time he shows his teeth making thin smile and nods. He pretends as if he is happy about seeing them.

Father of suicide person makes loud exclamation of happiness seeing Media Guy:

"Oh!!! For the first time in my life I see real Hero! That's great! I must shake hands with you, Hero."

Media Guy is frightened due to his painful arms, tries to make father of Suicide person not to shake hands: "Oh, Thank you… No, no, no…. Please, don't do it."

Father of suicide person confused: "Why, not? Hero… You deserve it… I have the honor to shake hands with you, my Hero, you save my son."

Father begins shaking hurt hands of Media Guy, who is not happy about that. Media Guy makes very painful, continuous, heartbreaking exclamation all time of shaking hands.

Media Guy cries: "No, Jesus… Please, help me… How lucky person I am:"

His pale face has painful grimace.

Father of Suicide person finishes shaking hands. Finally, mother of Suicide person does her part of family gratitude ceremony.

Mother of suicide person approach to Media Guy bed. She is very happy to see savior of her son, real hero: "You saved the life of my only son." No, for sure, there is no way to express gratitude. Yes… In today's world people like you have been almost disappeared. I've made some chicken soup, tomato sauce and cakes for you… Great man… Hero!"

Media Guy happy for absence of shaking hands as expression of gratitude. *Soup and cakes are better than shaking hands*, he thinks in himself trying to stop her long monologue: "Yes, yes... I see... Well, I am hero. Thank you."

Mother of suicide person continues in pathetic way, her eyes blinking: "I would like that my daughters marry man like you. Man who is like knight, with great heart and courage."

Media Guy thinks for himself, *I cannot marry two women. Lady, you have two daughters, not one.*

Mother of suicide person still speaking: "I'll hand a small gift to you personally, Hero... It small compensation for such courage."

She begins searching her bag. After a while she pulls out small dishes. Unfortunately, she drops dishes with chicken soup and tomato sauce spilling it on Media Guy. His face and shoulders are red and yellow he is poured with sticky soup and sauce. Seeing what she has done mother of Suicide person apologizes to Media Guy.

"Oh, I am awfully sorry, Hero... Please forgive me... I'm a bit confused... I've never seen Hero alive... Forgive me... Hero, Mother of suicide person says shocked by what she has just done.

Two sisters are holding pen, waiting for autograph. They ask confused Media Guy in one voice: "We need your autograph... We desperately need that autograph... Please. Hero!"

Sticky Media Guy, who has been poured by soup an sauce seconds ago, is not in good mood. However, he takes pen and small notebook from sisters and deliver his signature to them.

Chapter 27

Media Guy is okay now. He is brushing teeth in bathroom of rented apartment. He is employed again and he does he job well; that makes him self-confident again. He looks at himself in bathroom mirror making funny faces during teeth brushing. Wireless telephone is ringing; Media Guy enters room to pick up receiver stile brushing his teeth.

Media Guy over phone while brushing teeth, his voice is different due to that:
"Yeah… Who is it?" On other side of phone line is Susan, his former girl, shy as if she is sorry about breaking up over phone: "Hello… How are you?"
She is very polite, voice, very melodic, now as if she tweets not speaks over phone.

Media Guy puts receiver between left shoulder and head returning to bathroom; takes position in front of bathroom mirror. Surprised but very formal, there is no love any more to her. She has been almost forgotten.

"Oh… Fine… Good… You? How are you, Susan", Media Guy in cold voice over phone.
Susan as if she apologizes to him over phone: "Nice… Listen to me…I was fool… I want to make an excuse to you…"
Media Guy as if he is surprised over phone: "Oh, really… Why?!? Are you sure you want to do that? I guess it was school example of break up."

Susan, voice full of guilty over phone: "Oh, yes... Absolutely... It was what you said. At hat point"

Media Guy is gurgling water then spits it out. All those sounds are heard over phone. He doesn't try to be polite: "Sorry... Sorry, Susan... I'm doing very important job – brushing my teeth... I keep my teeth good. Dentists charge high rate, you know."

Susan over phone: "Oh, no... Doesn't matter... Hmm... I want to see you... As soon as possible...

Media Guy pretends as if he is astonished and shocked, over phone: "To see me. But, why? Oh, oh... Really... What did you say? Didn't you find another boy?

Susan as if she is ashamed over phone, tries to make him interested in her: "I want to see you as soon as possible... Please, we can arrange it."

Media Guy continues his task, still brushing teeth: "But why??? I guess there was the end of love story. Break up. End. That's all folks regarding you and me. Isn't it?"

Susan over phone, voice is trembling as if she is confused begging for forgiveness: "Yes, I want you... I want you to be my boy again... Believe me. I made terrible mistake." She starts sobbing.

Media Guy over phone still brushing teeth, ironic: "Hey, hey. Honey... Sorry, my former Honey, wasn't that you who has broken up... Didn't you tell, quoting I do not want to live with guy on welfare...Wasn't that you who told."

He quotes her words: "I need as every woman support. What support could man on social assistance offer woman"... Yes, these words are yours... not mine. Can't you remember what you said."

Susan over phone asking for forgiveness, sobbing: "Yes... I was wrong... terribly wrong... Please, forgive me." You have never been wrong in your whole life,"

Media Guy still merciless over phone: "Oh, really... Have I ever been wrong. That's none of your business. You were wrong over break up...That's was your idea, not mine. No chance... However, you are good looking smart girl. You'll find somebody... The world is full of rich guys... Then go! Go and pick somebody up...Grab the happiness."

Susan over phone, sad, trembling voice asking for forgiveness: "Please, please forgive me... I'll do whatever you want my Love."

Media Guy keep his ironic style: "Oh, no... What am I? Your Love... Please, don't call me your love. Oh, Jesus, I am so struck by your pathetic words. What hypocrisy. No... No chance at all...Bye, by an good luck."

He finishes phone talk putting receiver of wireless phone on shut toilet bowl. Media Guy sticks out his tongue at bathroom mirror saying to himself:

"No... No chance, Honey... It's over definitely over."

Chapter 28

Media Guy with Head of Wild Animals Association in TV studio talks about saving endangered species of wild animals. Studio is full of animals – two monkeys, small koala, tiger baby, two squirrels and two not too long pythons.

At the beginning most animals are unusually calm but as time passing they get restless. Head of Wild Animals Association is mid-aged fat woman with tons of make-up on her face. She holds tiger baby on lap giving him milk from small flask. Next to her armchair two pythons lie curled up. Close to Media Guy armchair is koala who sits on the floor eating some plant. Finally monkeys clothed in multicolor short pants are in front of round table which is located in the center of the studio. Monkeys have some toys in hands playing with them. For now everything is under control, almost perfect. Animals don't disrupt TV broadcasting. Show is no air.

Media Guy is trying to hide his animosity to animals. Frankly he is forced by Editor in Chief to make this TV program. He is speaking to Head of Wild Animals Association: "Well... Hmm... Please, tell us about your organization... Your projects... Goals... Future plans."

Head of Wild Animals Association replies sharply prepared answers: "By protecting Wildlife we protect nature and human beings as well... Industrialization without control means nothing... Many species simply disappeared due to people nonchalance."

Media Guy is interrupting her not to let become anchor: "I see… And what are your proposals to save and to protect wildlife?"

Head of Wild Animals Association continues sharply, loud and self-confident:
"Yeah… Good question… Simply to bring process of industrialization under control… Almost each single day some oil cargo ship or oil platform sinks causing death of many birds, seals and fishes in ocean… Crime hunters kill elephants and threatened species for earning big money on black market."

Media Guy is interrupting her again: "Well… Do you mean that police forces must do their job better… To punish those hunters and irresponsible companies involved in that dirty job? To imprison them, for instance."
"Yes, for sure… Those crooks must be in jails… Those bastards must be punished severely for such crime, she says.
Monkeys start crying as if they support Head of Wild Animals Association.
"They cash lives of wild innocent animals and become rich. If we are real human beings we must act properly and crime hunters must be arrested… That's the only way we must do," she continues exposing her ideas over threatened species and all animals, in general.

Media Guy is nodding head as sign of appovement: "Yeahh… I agree… But, don't you think there are some other options than putting people in jails… For instance… training and teaching them not to do such things."

Head of Wild Animals Association sharply replies: "Oh, no... That option takes much time...It's long, very long run. Using teaching & training option

Wildlife could disappear within several decades. We must... I shall repeat once more. We do must act as Emergency Task Force... It's very urgent... Believe me. Otherwise animals will be exterminated by the end of this century."

Growing support of animals in studio becomes obvious. Pythons start slow moving their heads and bodies, koala is walking around round table, tiger baby tries to leave Head's lap and monkeys start jumping through the studio while crying loudly. Seeing animals Media Guy figures out he will lose control over situation very soon. Therefore he gets afraid almost frightened. His face looks shocked. Actually, he has fear of snakes. Pythons start slow creeping towards Media Guy. Squirrels are jumping through studio on round tables, cameras etc... It's really funny sight, almost like in zoo.

Head of Wild Animals Association behaves very calm as if nothing is happening in studio, continues speaking: "Yeah... I've almost forgotten. Multinational companies... Hmm... Dirty business of ongoing raising profits... They trade animals, or their parts. They kill them as much as they can for the sake of bloody money."

Media Guy frightened of animals tries to change a topic of conversation, he expects some animal attack, for there are some dangerous species in studio.

He says: "I think we'd better not talk about multinational companies... Actually... We are here to see how to protect animals... Not to discuss companies' policy and business strategy... This is not economic forum."

Media Guy starts intensive sweating; drops on his face are visible. It gets very unpleasant for unusual studio guests.

Head of Wild Animals Association speaks text learned by heart: "Oh, no. No... You are not right. Multinational companies are big evil as sources of water, land and air pollution."

Animals are so restless that seems TV show is quite close to its end. One of two monkeys overturns two glasses of juice located on round table; other monkey is on the top of Media Guy head cheerfully showing teeth as winner. One of pythons is on the round table, another is close to armchair of Media Guy. Koala is climbing up reflector stand. Even cameraman gets nervous over such happening.

Head of Wild Animals Association very calm as if nothing is happening. Tiger baby is not in her lap any longer but walks through studio.

"Many animals are threatened by irresponsible acting of those multinationals. And... In my opinion, Multinationals CEO-s must be punished severely. They should be in prison too like poachers." She speaks.

Media Guy is so frightened as if he sees own death; his face is totally pale, lips tremble, eyes red, his body is shaking: "Wweell... Let's focus ourselves to the point. Let multinational companies put aside."

Head of Wild Animals Association doesn't bothered by animals walking and jumping in studio: "Focus?!? Focus on what? What are you talking about? Hey, do not protect your sponsors Media Shit!"

She gets angry for the first time during interview: "Each single day those VIPs kill rare species by so called accidents. And you protect them, bastard. Of course they sponsor media, they pay you. That's why you protect them."

Media Guy seeing and feeling python climbing up to his left leg he faints gets frightened to death as never so far.

Head of Wild Animals Association surprised by fainted Media Guy; looking at him in half-lying position in his luxurious armchair. Python's head is on Media Guy chest at this point. No matter what's going on in studio she continues:

"Jesus... Media adore their sponsors... Hmm... Strange, How much media love its sponsors, more than anything else. All for the sake of fucking money. Bullshit," she says breathing out deeply.

Chapter 29

Dinner at Media Guy parents home; pleasant atomsphere. Media Guy parents are very proud of their son – TV superstar. There are several dishes on the dinning table – soup, two kinds of salads, chops with smashed potatoes and nice fruitcake. Mother, father and Media Guy are sitting at the dinning table eating soup. Obviously they all, really, enjoy meal.

Mother to Media Guy: "How do you like this soup... This was your favorite soup when you were kid. I prepared it to you exclusively. You have asked for another plate of soup very often... Haven't you remembered?"

Media Guy eating soup: "Yes, mummy... You are right. That was my favorite dish...More precisely – one of favorites."

Mother looks happy evokes his son childhood, her eyes are bright: "Well...Hmm... You see this banana & mango fruitcake. That was the main reason you were putting on weight... Yes, my son."

Media Guy is focused to delicious soup, keeps on eating: "Yes, mummy... Again... You are quite right."

Father to Media Guy: "Our son... Our pride... But I want you get married."

Hearing those words Media Guy chokes up.

"I'm an old man and I want to see my grandson... or granddaughter, never mind, before I die. Isn't it quite natural. Do I ask too much from you," Father says making deep sigh.

Media Guy is getting a little bit nervous over father's statement: "Shit! Sorry mother for this word... But... Father is boring. I have dinner. It's not time for hard topics and hard talk. My dad, let me enjoy this meal."

Mother is not happy by such father's remarks and warns him: "Yeah... Stop boring my son... Let him enjoy dinner. Today is not right time for such talks."

Father seeing he cannot force others to accept his topic gets nervous: "Yes, yes... Any... Literally, any question of mine is disturbing. Okay, do whatever you want. I will shut up my mouth."

Mother arguing with father: "Yes... Any question... In particular if it's stupid."

Father still keeping his way of talking, to mother: "Yeah...But our son is 41... Don't you think he is old enough to get married...He is not teenager. People at his age have children who attend primary school."

Media Guy throwing spoon in the plate with soup as if he gets angry. To parents: "Hey, hey stop! Do not quarrel over me, please... I beg you, my dear parents. I do not want to see you like that. I want happy, smiling parents."

Mother accepts her son's proposal: "You are right dear son... Let's talk about... About... I have no idea... Help me son."

Media Guy is honored of giving final words, gets very serious: "Let's talk about nothing... We'd better go eating these delicious dishes... As far as I am concerned that would be optimal solution at this point." All present people start smiling.

Media Guy parents are now cheerful. They accept his suggestion: "Yeah... Let's all go eating."

Chapter 30

Nice and big City park; Media Guy strolls through the City park listening to the Discman music with earphones on his head. At the same time he is reading some newspaper, which are fully stretched so he can hardly see the way in front of him.

From time to time he stops for the moment focusing him to some important article in newspaper. As the outcome of good Discman music Media Guy gradually starts to make rhythmical moves shaking and turning over his body, arms, legs and head. Frankly, it looks very funny. Seeing a small boy flying kite Media Guy instantly puts newspaper together roughly pulling out flying kite from kid's hands. Media Guy getting happy about having flying kite starts running away.

Kid is crying: "Give me my kite, Give me my kite." Angry kid with tears in eyes starts running after Media Guy. At that point Media Guy figures out what terrible mistake he has made and returns flying kite to kid.

Media Guy is apologizing to kid: "I'm sorry... Awfully sorry...Shame on me!"

Kid is still weeping but gradually gets calm. Suddenly kid kicks Media Guy to his knee.

Media Guy makes painful cry: "Ooouucchh! Shit! Oh, sorry for dirty words... Okay, okay... I am guilty... Crime and Punishment... You are the winner... And I am loser." Kid stops weeping starring at Media Guy as if he is nut. Media Guy takes his wallet, pulls out 20 bucks giving it to small boy. After that he keeps on solo walking through the City Park. After short walk he sits on a bench.

Media Guy enjoys leisure time; to himself: "Hmm... Beautiful day... I like days off duty... Hmmm..." He is happy about not working anything, he looks at the blue sky and pigeons pecking some particles of bread near the bench where he is seated. At that point mobile phone is ringing. He jumped as he was thunderstruck.

"Shit... Who is it!?! Who breaks my enjoying leisure," Media Guy says furiously. He takes mobile phone from inside pocket of his jacket: "Yes. Who are you."

Editor in Chief is on other side of phone line: "How are you Media Star? I have assignment for you. It's tailored exactly for you."

Media Guy disappointed due to fact he must rush to work, cynical over mobile phone: "Really!?! That must be something great...historical... Likely that nobody is willing to do... except me... crazy Media Guy."

Editor in Chief is getting bored with Media Guy cynicism over mobile phone: "Please, do not talk to me that way... Last month you were paid third best salary... You are not underpaid, but overpaid. That's me and deputy who got more money than you... Am I clear! I guess there is no choice!"

Media Guy as if accepts normal way of talking but still very reluctant: "Okay, okay... Due to you I will soon be as rich as Bill Gates... for instance... Lucky me, I'll be billionaire." He bursts in laughter.

Editor in Chief surprised and slightly disappointed by Media Guy acting: "Very, very funny. You'll never be mature... Okay, listen to me carefully... There is big Italian circus in the city."

Media Guy obviously not happy about this assignment: "Yes... My ears are stuck to mobile... So what... I don't go to circus."

Editor in Chief continues over mobile phone: "Yeah, I know…But young tiger fled an hour ago…Pardon, half hour ago…tiger is seen near the City Park."

Media Guy frightened starts choking and stuttering over mobile phone: "Wh… Wh… What did you say!?! City Park! Shit! I'm in City Park at this point…Oh, Jesus… My life is threatened."

Editor in Chief makes exclamation of sudden happiness: "Great!!! I'm sending TV crew to the City Park right now… Stay where you are… Don't move anywhere. Do you understand? Yooppiee… You are lucky guy… Don't you understand you are lucky! You take exclusive stuff only." Editor in Chief finishes mobile phone talk.

Media Guy frightened throws mobile phone behind bench. Sudden roaring of some beast is heard. Media Guy completely pale as if he is dead not alive turns behind back to see what happens. Tiger is lying approximately 25 to 30 feet behind the bench on which Media Guy is sitting. Media Guy mobile phone hit the tiger. But despite that tiger is unusually calm playing with mobile phone like a cat. Seeing beast close to him Media Guy faints and falls on the grass.

Chapter 31

Nice, rather luxurious restaurant in downtown; Media Guy and elegant pretty lady, blonde, age 35 or so are sitting waiting to order some dish and drink. In the meantime they are chatting. Atmosphere in restaurant is very friendly. In one corner pianist, older man with moustaches and glasses plays the piano. Music is slow rhythm. Blonde lady is employed with big Media Company as Public Relations Manager – PR Lady.

Media Guy talks to PR Lady who resembles more to supermodel than office clerk: "Well. I guess this place is very nice for such kind of meeting. Atmosphere is really pleasant."

PR Lady keeps official style of conversation: "You are quite right… You know…Today it's very important… I mean in the age of crime… However, this city area is very safe. I have never seen in media something bed had happened in this district."

Media Guy approves with easy nodding: "Yeah… Exactly. You told me you had something to ask me!?!"

PR Lady looks straight at Media Guy eyes: "Yes… Well… Actually our company is willing to hire you… You are Media Star… And we are ready to meet your financial requirements."

Media Guy is suddenly surprised by her statement: "Pardon… You won't me to work for you?!?"

PR Lady replies sharply: "Exactly. For our company. Is it possible?

Media Guy is slightly confused, thinks whether is so good professional that companies are ready to fight for him. He replies in indecisive voice: "Well. Hmm… I have to talk to my Editor In Chief first… You know. That's how it works in the United States."

PR Lady keeps official style of negotiating: "Well… I see… We are ready to compensate your company too… Nobody would worry on money." Waiter approaching table for order.

Waiter: "Good evening dear guests… May I have your order, please."

PR Lady and Media Guy almost in one voice: "Good evening, Sir… We'll tell you right now. Please, wait a second." Both are looking at menu.

PR Lady to waiter: "Smoked Salmon with sea salad… And wine… Red wine, of course… I like it very much. Hmm. More precisely I adore it."

She smiles and focus her eyes again to Media Guy: "What do you want Media Star?"

Media Guy to waiter: "Yeah. Same… the same for me."

Waiter checks order: "Well…Your order is – Two smoked salmons with sea salads and bottle of our branded archive red wine… Okay… Have a nice evening."

After taking order waiter leaves their table.

PR Lady talks with wide pleasant smile: "Okay… Let's go back to our negotiations…you can work for both companies… We don't mind it. That can be arranged too if you want it."

Media Guy as if he gets nervous: "Okay, okay… you don't mind it… But I don't really know whether my present boss will mind it… He must agree to."

Pianist plays the piano. Fine piano music and guests murmur in the background of the scene. Nobody expects something very bad is coming soon. Suddenly four terrorists break into the restaurant all with machine guns and black masks on their heads. Guests frightened to death start horrible screaming; shortly after that one of the terrorists fires a couple of bursts into air. Guests start falling to the floor trying to escape the worst. Now, all guests are lying on the restaurant floor with faces down. All terrorists are in camouflage clothing.

Terrorist A is screaming to frighten restaurant guests: "Okay… Listen to me carefully… This is not robbery… We are looking for exact person… We just want to take him… So be calm. And, of course, strictly follow and act in accordance to our orders."

Terrorist B in threatening voice: "We must clarify. No heroes here and now.No, heroes… Please! You know where most heroes end."

Terrorist C very loudly: "And everything will be Okay!!! In other words. Obey the rules, and orders and all will stay alive and completely healthy in good mood."

Terrorist D speaks same way, very loudly: "You will be perfectly safe! Again… No heroes, please!!!"

Media Guy is under tablecloth not on floor as other guests with faces down. Complete silence in restaurant. In a moment Media Guy starts bad coughing.

Terrorist A at that point fires a burst into restaurant window. Sound of glass breaking is heard. Short guests screams are heard too, then complete silence except Media Guy coughing.

"So… It seems that there is a hero here," Terrorist A says approaching to table under which Media Guy is hidden; then removes tablecloth by machine gun.

Seeing Media Guy on knees Terrorist A says to him: "That's you… Hero… Brave man, what are you doing here. The order was: Lye on the floor with face down."

Terrorist B comes closer to Media Guy, very surprised, almost shocked seeing him as if he finds wanted person: "Hmm… That must be him… Just a moment." He is looking at small photo in hand then at Media Guy. Terrorist B repeats that procedure of cross-looking at photo and Media Guy several times.

Terrorist A surprised: "That's… That's who?"

Terrorist B sharply replies: "That's him. Yes, that's him. Man we are looking for!"

Terrorist C makes cheerful exclamation: "Okay… Let's take him and run away from here as soon as possible! Within seconds. I don't wont to welcome Police Emergency Squad."

All four terrorists with machine guns aimed at Media Guy pull out him and take him away in the unknown direction. They are leaving the restaurants with Media Guy hand cuffed.

Chapter 32

Isolated, small cottage on wooded hill is the place where Media Guy is taken away. At this point camera doesn't show exterior that looks as if it's far away from any civilization. Interior of cottage quite unknown to Media Guy. He is sitting on leather armchair with handcuff locked. Across from him one terrorist with machine gun is sitting in sofa. That terrorist is in charge of keeping Media Guy. Very tense situation. Terrorists took Media Guy mobile phone and his documents. terrorist is completely masked, Media Guy frightened to death for he as journalist knows what terrorist usually do their victims. They torture severely kidnapped persons, then kill in very cruel way. It could be beheading, putting victim in cage with hunger tiger or in room with highly venomous snakes or bugs.

Shit, That is the end I have never deserved. Jesus, Why me. What so bad and wrong I have done, thinks Media Guy.

Terrorist looking at wallet they took from Media Guy; disappointed to Media Guy: "Hmm... 73 bucks... Obviously, you don't like cash... You probably prefer credit cards. You are not poor man."

Media Guy doesn't know what terrorist is talking about to him: "What do you mean? I don't like cash. I don't understand your statement."

Terrorist is very surprised by Media Guy question, if he gets angry: "What do I mean?!? You ask me... What do I mean... Millionaire with 73 bucks in his pocket... Isn't it ridiculous? We did not kidnap man on welfare."

Media Guy now even more confused, cannot figure out what's going on, to terrorist: "What are you talking about. What millionaire? I'm not millionaire... Hmm, just ordinary man... You, probably have more money than me."

Terrorist bursts in laughter, ironic to Media Guy: "Oh, really... You are not rich, but poor. The owner of multinational petrol company must be a poor guy... Very touching... Oh, Jesus help me believe it."

Media Guy seeing terrorists kidnapped wrong person tries to clarify some facts: "The owner of multinational petrol company!?! Very funny... I am a poor journalist... I'm not rich man... I earn slightly above minimum wage."

Terrorist gets angry, loud: "You... You are not rich... What liar you are."

He is coming very close to Media Guy pulls out a couple of photos from one of outside pockets and shows them: "Who is this? This Guy on yacht..."

Media Guy looks at photos seeing striking similarity of that person to him; as if they are twins:

"Maybe, some orphan", terrorist says cynically smiling.

Media Guy tries to tell the truth: "Yeah...That man is almost like me. But, you are wrong...That's not me... Believe me... You can check it... Call my office... Call my parents... Or, you can check my bank account..."

Media Guy mobile phone is ringing. Terrorist puts photos in pocket and returns to sofa to turn off Media Guy mobile phone.

Terrorist keeps cynical way of talking: "Hmm…Call the office… Call the parents…Check my bank accounts… What bastard you are! You are richer than many small countries in Asia and Africa taking alone! Do you happen to know that almost half of world population is hungry… literally hungry! They are happy to see a loaf of bread."

Media Guy gets very nervous: "So what… What can I do about it. Listen to me carefully… I am not the boss of any petrol company… I am… As simple as that… Journalist with average salary. Can you understand it."

Terrorist smiling; doesn't believe Media Guy words: "Bullshit! You want me believe you… (pause) Hmm… Funny… You think I am an idiot, don't you."

Media Guy seeing big Lenin picture on the wall; almost shocked: "Wh… Wha… What's this!?! Why is this picture on the wall. Do you really follow him."

Terrorist can't make out what Media Guy asks: "I don't understand you… What's your problem? You have some objection regarding this picture on the wall. Why."

Media Guy as if is getting angry: "Shame on you! How dare you. However, in my opinion you are just bloody terrorists… No matter you have Lenin on your wall… Great revolutionary."

Terrorist at that point bursts into anger: "Hey, hey man! Please, do not talk to me that way!" He is coming very close to Media Guy, obviously in rage, waving machine gun as if he wants to hit Media Guy in the head: "We are… Listen to me carefully! We are revolutionaries! Not terrorists! Bastard! That's you who are thief, crook and bloodsucker billionaire."

Media Guy is losing control, angry and loudly: "Hmm... You... Revolutionaries! You must be kidding! Kidnapping people is not the way of revolutionizing the world! That's, nothing more and less, than pure crime and terror over people."

Terrorist is returning to his sofa not so angry as if he has been: "No, no... No you are wrong." It looks as if he accepts dialogue with Media Guy.

"We need money for making the world better... Just a few wealthy families keep almost all world assets... That's not just, isn't it. So... We kidnap only very rich people, not ordinary, or even middle class people," terrorist says trying to explain his mission.

Media Guy nodding, cynical: "Oh, really... You need money... Everybody needs money... That's common as breathing the air...So go ahead get some job, not kidnap people."

Terrorist keeps serious teaching style, keeps explaining their job: "Exactly. Everybody needs money... But... Due to few very greedy people, like you, for instance, most of us have miserable lives...work 10 hours for miserable wages, cannot afford decent education and quality healthcare."

Media Guy smiling: "Me? Greedy... Please, Let's get serious... Journalist with average income greedy... Foolish!"

Terrorist continues the same way: "Very interesting... Boss of big multinational petrol company with average income... It's really amusing with you...Oh, God, let me believe this idiot!" He bursts in laughter.

Media Guy fearful for armed terrorist who doesn't believe him anything: "Okay. I agree. Why don't you check my bank accounts if you don't believe me. I swear I do not have money you want...

Terrorist with ear to ear wide cynical smile: "Oh, yes...You do have...You do have more money than we want to keep you alive... Let's say... 10,000,000 bucks in cash...Not too much to stay alive...Isn't it?"

Media Guy at this point is getting an idea of using his special Rolex watch in state of emergency. He hopes it will work. To terrorist: "I must go pissing...Tell me where is the toilet?"

Terrorist replies cynically: "You are really strange guy... I talk about revolution... And, at that point, you must pee... Jesus, what kind of man you are?!?"

Media Guy sharply: "What can I do... Forces of nature still dominate human being... I guess, you pee sometimes too. Am I right?"

Terrorist nervous: "Okay, okay... Just go pissing..." He comes to Media Guy unlocking handcuff then follows him to toilet with machine gun aimed at him.

Chapter 33

Terrorist stays in front of closed toilet door holding machine gun. He is aware that Media Guy cannot escape at any way, otherwise he would be killed by his friends.

Media Guy is in toiled behind closed door; nervous speaking to his watch silently:
"Let's go...Let's go honey... Yes you can do it." He is still touching and pushing buttons on the watch as if he searching for some kind of panic button.
Terrorist to Media Guy through closed door: "Hey, rich... Have you finished your pissing... Hurry up. You don't give a speech at Economic Forum."
Media Guy to terrorist through closed door: "No... Not yet... I do my best to finish peeing as soon as possible. I have some problems with prostate."

Yes... Yooppiee... SOS works, Media Guy thinks. On the small watch screen is written in striking red color letters "EMERGENCY CONNECTION ESTABLISHED".
Terrorist surprised to Media Guy: "Are you okay rich... You are happy about pissing...Hmm... Don't jerk. Masturbation is not allowed here, just pissing. No pleasures, please."

Media Guy tries to hide the cause of sudden happiness. However he was the best talent for acting in high school: "Ouch! My poor cock..."

Terrorist very surprised: "Oh... What about your cock?!? What have you done stupid rich?"

Media Guy sharply replies: "Zipper gets jammed my cock..." He makes painful scream and painful grimace.

Terrorist to Media Guy through closed door: "Do you need some help, rich?"

Media Guy almost shocked refusing help: "Oh, no... No... Thank you anyway... That's very kind of you... But so far my private parts have been matter of women interests... Can't you understand it... Well, thank you again..."

Terrorist now polite: "You are welcome rich..."

City Police Department Emergency Electronic Control Unit. Many policemen and other staff sitting in front of computer screens starring at display. Policemen are looking at computer screen with extreme attention.

One Policeman suddenly cries: "Hey, guys! Let's go! This man must be in really big trouble... Let's help him immediately! I will alarm Emergency Task Unit."

Policeman who noticed SOS message from Media Guy makes emergency call to special Police Antiterrorist Department.

Chapter 34

Small cottage where kidnapped Media Guy is located. Now all four terrorists, each with machine gun are in the room with Media Guy. Terrorists eat pizzas and drink some beer. Media Guy with handcuff is watching them.

Terrorist A suddenly to others: "Hey, hey! I've almost forgotten there is NBA basket ball match on TV… We must see it… We cannot miss it. That's great show."

Terrorists B, C, D together in one voice: "You are right… Turn on TV… Terrorist A leaves sofa, approaches TV in the corner turning it on. All terrorists starts looking at TV broadcasting NBA basketball match as if they are completely hypnotized.

Terrorist B enjoying sport show and eating pizza: "Hmm… This pizza is delicious… Basket ball match too. Pleasure for mind and stomach."

Terrorist C to Media Guy: "Do you want pizza, rich? It's really good with ham and mushrooms. Do you like mushrooms? I adore it."

Media Guy makes official polite refusal: "No… No thank you… I am not hungry…"

Seeing that Media Guy doesn't want their company Terrorist D to Media Guy: "Oh, yes… You are hungry… But… Pizza slices are not in accordance with your eating style… I guess you prefer open seas food and… archive wines, of course… Meals on private yacht… Hmm… Am I right rich?" All terrorist burst in laughter.

Media Guy sharply replies: "No! You are not right at all! I like pizzas, but I am not hungry at this point. Can't you understand it."

Approximately 100 feet from cottage antiterrorist police squad of 15 policemen tries to find the best way to rescue Media Guy. Sky is clear. Stars bright. Wonderful night for romantic experience not antiterrorist action. Head of Antiterrorist Squad is looking at his small palmtop electronic device for a while. Seeing exact coordinates on small color screen of palmtop turns to other policemen.

Cheerful but rather silent voice to others: "Let's go guys…We are a step towards executing this task… Let's show those sons of bitches what Emergency Task Force really is… Go Ahead."
Others greeting their boss all together but not too loud for this is covert mission:
"Yeah… Let's do it… Come on, smash the crooks."

Terrorists are hypnotized and cheerful looking at NBA basketball match on TV; on other side Media Guy looks desperate starring through empty air.

Terrorist A cheerful voice: "Hey… We'll be rich when we get 10,000,000 bucks in cash for Petrol Guy. I will retire, I need some time to enjoy life, not just to kidnap rich bastards." He starts whistling melody Money makes the World go round.
Terrorist B sharply: "Yeah! Just imagine 10,000,000 on a pile… I am eager to see it… Yuppie! We are rich men!"
Terrorist C happy up, up to the sky: "Just imagine… Yacht… Tropical Sea… and… the most important of all!"

Terrorist D shares cheerful mood with comrades: "Chicks... Babes.... Girls... Beautiful women... Doesn't matter... All work...Oh." He makes deep passionate sigh. Suddenly strong sound of cracking is heard. Terrorists get frightened to death, Media Guy not. For him that's sign of hope.

Terrorist A gets extremely pale as if he is dead: "Oh, Jesus! This must be earthquake!"

Terrorist B frightened too, voice is trembling: "Ye... Yea... Yeah... Unfortunately, this area is well known for disastrous earthquakes! Are, we so happy?"

Terrorist C frightened to death tries to comfort himself and others: "Oh, no... I do hope these moments are not last in our lives!" He suddenly bursts in tears. Two big cracks are made on the ceiling of the room. Through those cracks two policemen from emergency squad are fallen. They are in antiterrorist uniforms with masks on heads. All terrorists are deeply shocked, more dead than alive.

Policeman A holding machine gun, very loudly: "Okay! All, hands up! High... high in the air! Imagine you want to touch the sky."

He turns to Media Guy, speaking to him: "Except you, dear friend... Come here, with me. These bastards will spend rest of their lives in prison." Media Guy comes close to Policeman A. Terrorists raise their hands high in the air.

Policeman B holding machine gun, directs it to terrorists, very loudly to them: "And! You dirty, four bastards on the floor immediately! Now!!! Imagine you kiss the floor. Passionate kiss, Please!" All terrorists immediately lie on the floor with face down stuck to the ground.

"No... Not good enough! Face down! I said, "Face down!" "Stuck to the floor. Imagine that instead of floor is young nude beautiful blonde," Policeman B says.
Terrorists execute the order sticking faces to the floor.

"That's much better! No moves! Stay that way! No heroes please, if you want stay alive", Policeman B says in threatening voice.

Soon other policemen, members of Emergency Task Force Unit, enter the room. All with masks on heads holding machine guns aimed at terrorists. One of them is handcuffing terrorists then unlocks Media Guy handcuff throwing it away.

Chapter 35

In the USFTV headquarters glamorous cocktail party is held in honor of multiple hero – Media Guy. There are more than hundred guests not counting USFTV staff. Atmosphere is very cheerful. Editor in chief delivers a short speech boasting Media Guy who stands next to him.

Editor in Chief ending his speech that is ode to Media Guy: "Finally... This mister" pointing at Media Guy and continues "is not only professional committed to the excellence, but... First of all good and brave man... We, all, me, colleagues, his friends and complete USFTV are proud of him." Very loud applause of almost all cocktail attendants. Media Guy takes microphone to thank Editor in Chief and all guests.

Media Guy is happy tries to thank all present people: "No, I won't make speech... I just want to thank you all... Thank you very much for support... You are great! I am really proud of you. Everything is easy with such support."

Among large number of present guests are media stars, journalists, writers, directors and local city politicians. Waiters serve guests; most guests hold a glass of wine, champagne or cocktail. They enjoy drinking.

At that point Emergency Antiterrorist Squad of 15 policemen, who saved Media Guy, enter the cocktail room. Guests greet them by intensive applauding. Policemen wearing regular uniforms walk single file. At the top is the

Head of Antiterrorist Squad. Hearing guests' applauding policemen wave arms.

Seeing them Media Guy makes cheerful exclamation
to policemen: "If you didn't save me I shouldn't be alive…
Oh, my God… My Saviors. God bless you."

Tears appear on his face. Media Guy was touched
directly to the heart by courage of those men.

Head of Antiterrorist Squad to Media Guy with smile:
"No, no… You are not right… We'll pay 10,000,000 bucks
for you anyway…You are definitely worth that money."

Chapter 36

It's night, Media Guy sleeps in bedroom of his apartment. He is dreaming nice dreams. Due to type of dreams his face looks happy with thin smile. Obviously he is very please by content of dreams. His dream – Long sand beach somewhere on Tropical Island; sapphire blue ocean in front of the beach, palm trees in background. Very nice sight. Media Guy wearing only bathing trunks and sun glasses sits in easy chair and enjoys exotic view of really extraordinary place.

Media Guy staring at high seas, to himself: "Hmm... This must be the Paradise... I cannot believe... Is this reality... Or, dream, maybe?" Media Guy is the only one at the beach. But it doesn't bother him, he is happy.

Media Guy smiling to himself, enjoys natural beauties unseen so far: "Now, I figure out what The Hell is. Office... Civilization... Cities... Bloody western lifestyle... That's the real Hell... Bullshit urban life."

Next to easy chair is small flask with cold lemonade. Media Guy takes it starting to drink: "Hmm... Cold lemonade... Fantastic..." Staring at high seas as if he is obsessed by that sight: "No words that could describe this beauty... No writer who can write on this. This is so unreal." While dreaming his face looks as if it is blessed.

Media Guy continues to himself in dreams: "No working hours... No chiefs... No duties... No subway crowded with office rats hurrying to work in neon light offices. On what craps we spend our only life."

At that point women giggling is heard somewhere in background. Three very beautiful girls, a brunette, a blonde and a redhead wearing very tight swimming suits are running towards Media Guy.

Media Guy seeing girls, more beautiful than sex bombs, suddenly makes long and loud scream of happiness: "Oh, Yippee. What babes! Real Paradise! No Paradise without chicks." Approaching Media Guy girls giggling touch all parts of his body, chests, hands, legs. He starts giggling due to intensive girls attack of titillating.

Media Guy a little bit ashamed but happy: "Hey, hey...Take it easy babes!"
Girls splash him with sun milk starting rubbing it over Media Guy body.
"Wow! Jesus...This is fantastic," he says to girls.
"Take it easy...Please honeys, I cannot stand such amount of pleasures," says Media Guy. Media Guy accepts this game and lets girls touching him "defending" himself by similar action - touching girls. It slowly slides to indecent group party with young girls.

Media Guy suddenly awakes from wonderful dream. He is in bedroom with wet face due to intensive dreams, he moves his hand to face to wipe drops of sweat.

Media Guy breaths out deep sigh of disappointment: "Oh, unfortunately this was only a dream...Shit!"

Chapter 37

Media Guy and Editor in Chief have a meal in Fast food restaurant, not luxurious – ordinary surroundings. Silent music is heard.

Editor in Chief drinking hot chocolate to Media Guy: "Hmm... This cup of black drink is healing."

Media Guy is chewing fish sandwich: "Yeah... Quite right... Sandwich is delicious too." He keeps on eating fish sandwich as if he doesn't want to be bothered with some other stuff.

Editor in Chief: "You've passed through terrible experience... I mean on kidnapping... How do you feel now? Do you have some problems?"

Media Guy makes thin official smile approving the statement: "Yeah... Terrible experience... But at this point... That's nothing more or less than pure past...Just a part of life history... Just that... To answer your questions. I feel pretty good and I haven't any problems, in particular, not regarding mental health."

Editor in Chief: "Yeah. It might be good for you to take a week or two off. To visit some exotic part of this damned world... Refreshing both your minds and body."

Media Guy welcomes this proposal: "Exactly... That's what I've wanted to ask you... Yeah, I must go to holiday... I desperately need it."

Editor in Chief is smiling: "Yeah... That's finished... Just do it... Call immediately tourist agency to book the trip... Go... Just go wherever you like... Enjoy each single minute."

Media Guy reacts cheerfully: "Yeah... It's done, my big boss." Both of them are smiling.

Editor in Chief suddenly remembers that he must do something important: "Yeahh. Shit. How I dare to forget it." He is slapping his own head: "I am senile. I've almost forgotten. Shame on me."

Media Guy suddenly gets worried, even afraid for he doesn't know what's going on: "Wh... Wha... What's that? Tell me!" He is expecting bad news, his face turns pale without the slightest smile

Editor in Chief puts right hand in inside pocket of his jacket pulling out white envelope: "Yeah... That's it... Very important stuff. And that is for you, young gentleman."

Media Guy still shocked – afraid of firing or some court indictment, so often in journalism, his experience hasn't been so good so far: "Ye... Yea... Yeah... What's that! Tell me, please." He looks straight at Editor in Chief; drops of sweat are rolling down his face; loud: "Tell me finally what's that! I'm so eager to know."

Editor in Chief smiles delivering white envelope to Media Guy: "Open it. Lucky Guy. Small reward from Chief Executive Official." He bursts in laughter.

Media Guy opens envelope and sees check on 15,000$ payable to him, *how generous from company*, he thinks at that point: "Yopiee! 15,000 bucks... It is like lottery win." He bursts in laughter making exclamation of happiness: "That is really good!!! Thank you my dear Editor in Chief, thank to CEO and all USFTV management. That's very kind of you."

Editor in Chief makes sincere historical smile, very rare and unusual for him: "As far as I am concerned, You deserve more... Top Gun."

Chapter 38

Movie stars don't want to be disturbed on public places. The same is with Media Guy, with huge sunglasses and funny hat jammed on head Media Guy sits at the international airport waiting for boarding call.

Voice from loudspeakers is calling passengers: "Last call for the flight 177 for Borneo."

Shortly upon hearing words *Last call for the flight 177* Media Guy stands up immediately moving towards exit to the aircraft. Due to big speed of this operation he falls breaking his huge sunglasses for identity protection. At that point several boys and girls recognized him; cheerful they make circle around Media Guy asking him for autograph.

Media Guy is standing up, nervous: "Okay, okay… But only a minute… I rush to board on plane." Cheerful people around him greet that suggestion, he starts giving autographs, then he boarded to plane for Borneo.

Interior of the aircraft. Plane flies high in the air; Media Guy with earphones on head makes rhythmic head moves as if he is enjoying music. Next to his seat is an old lady who looks at him as if he is crazy. He keeps on making funny head moves and funny faces not caring about anyone.

Media Guy is spreading some magazine, to himself: "Let's see what Paradise looks like." He is opening pages with exotic pictures of his holiday destination. There are nude women on some pictures but not offensive. Old lady, sitting next to him, obviously gets very disturbed by Media Guy behavior and nude images.

"Yeah...Ten days in Paradise... Yoopie," Media Guy exclaims.

Old lady now shocked, to herself: "Oh, my Lord... I sit next to sin-maker... Oh, Lord...Forgive me... Forgive him."

Media Guy figures out he must change behavior, to old lady: "Oh sorry...I'm awfully sorry... Dear lady, please forgive me." At that point he stops making funny moves and puts closed magazine in the seat pocket in front of him.

Chapter 39

Media Guy is on the airport close to his holiday destination. On his head is big sombrero with U.S. flag imprinted in upper part and huge sunglasses on nose. He is looking for some taxicab. Finally he approaches to big black limousine then enters. Taxicab driver is fat black man in dark blue uniform with cap. Media Guy is sitting on rear seats.

Media Guy polite to taxicab driver: "Good afternoon… Golden Bay… Hotel "Exotic", please."

Taxicab driver surprised, cheerful: "Lucky man. You are so lucky." He looks at Media Guy in rear mirror: "That's real paradise, You'll enjoy, believe me."

Media Guy talks to taxicab driver, it's usual exchange of words in such occasions: "Oh… I'm glad to hear it… Maybe it's a bit exaggerated."

Taxicab driver riding limousine and talking to Media Guy: "Oh, no… That's true… There is no place in the whole world like Golden Bay. You'll be fascinated." He speaks as if he is obsessed by it: "Sea, Sand and Sun are nowhere on the globe so fantastic… Nowhere. It's Paradise on Earth."

Media Guy now gets cheerful: "Really… I am happy about that! Yes I do."

Taxicab driver: "You'll see the Paradise soon…It's about 25 miles from the airport…You'll be there within 10 to 15 minutes if everything go well."

Black limousine is sliding along the highway at normal speed. On both sides of the highway is real jungle. It looks like as if the highway breaks the quiet of wildlife nature as if it's not in accordance to jungle rules.

Taxicab driver is trying to make atmosphere friendlier: "What do you do for living? I hope you don't mind this question."

Media Guy replies sharply: "Oh, no. Why should I. Well I am journalist employed with TV… Nothing spectacular."

Taxicab driver surprised, makes exclamation: "Oh, yes. Journalist. That's fantastic job… What about me… You see I'm a miserable taxicab driver… I'll never be famous." He makes deep sigh of disappointment unhappy about his life.

Harsh sudden sound of brakes is heard. In front of limousine there is a couple of huge logs on the highway.

Taxicab driver furious, loudly: "Shit!!! Again those fucking tribes… Sorry for dirty words."

He and Media Guy get out of the car going towards logs. At that point very sharp thin arrows are stuck into logs. Shortly after that about 30 members of a wild tribe emerge from the wood next to the highway surrounding Media Guy and taxicab driver who are confused and shocked. All clothes on their thin muscle black bodies are small slips made of leaves. Their bodies are painted with various colors according to their tradition. Operation of coming to the highway and surrounding is accompanied by strange screams; upon that they start talking to taxicab driver in extremely strange language. Taxicab driver at that point turns translator. More precisely he talks to head of tribe group.

Taxicab driver confused to Media Guy: "They want you."

Media Guy has no idea what's this all about, frightened to taxicab driver: "Why? Why they want me? I don't understand."

Taxicab driver replies: "Frankly, neither do I. But... The reason is – quotation – "An American crap"... They are anti-American tribe... And they don't like you... More precisely they hate you. Why didn't you take off that hat with U.S. flag?!? They saw flag and now... You are in great trouble."

Media Guy afraid of wild tribe, He was told many horrible things about savages: "So what... What can I do... Yes, the hell, I'm American... And due to that they could terrorize me... Shit!"

Taxicab driver: "Just follow their instructions... Hmm... Actually I must tell you... You are in tribe custody. That's very bad indeed."

Media Guy makes strong exclamation of despair: "Shit... How lucky I am."

At that point he is pulling out his pocket trying to give some money to wild people in order to get rid of them.

Taxicab driver warns Media Guy: "Oh, no. No, don't do it... They hate U.S. money... According to them it's the perfect mean of humiliation. Don't act American way. No use doing it."

Members of wild tribe armed themselves with bows and arrows. All time they chat in some strange language.

Taxicab driver explains to Media Guy: "I know that's the way Americans do but... (pause) I must warn you they are ready to use force if needed... Please, the best would be to follow their instructions... And... Arrows are poisoned."

Media Guy drives mad, loudly: "Yes, yes... This is Paradise... where some savages will kill me... Oh, Jesus... Help me, please! I have never dreamed to end my life this way!" He is looking at the blue sky, bursts in cry. Savages stay calm looking agony of a typical white man from the great, great West.

Chapter 40

Nice Dream.

Media Guy is sitting on the deck of luxurious yacht drinking some cocktail through straw. He is staring at high seas enjoying the life for real and wearing exclusive extravagant sunglasses and shirt without sleeves with image of tiger.

Media Guy takes magazine from the small table next to him starting looking at pictures of almost nude girls: "Oh… This must be the Paradise." He is looking at high seas.

"Mother nature is creator of this beauty." Media Guy says and looks at girls in magazine.

"However, this beauty is created by nature too… Hmm." Media Guy comments images of seminude girls in magazine. He makes deep sigh of pleasure, smiling.

Suddenly three extremely beautiful girls – all natural blondes in very tight bikinis circle Media Guy starting to touch and caress him. While caressing him girls giggle in typical women way. Girls start rubbing their bodies against Media Guy body in very direct way, even indecently.

Media Guy makes very deep sigh of extraordinary pleasure: "Hmm… This is the double… Oh, no… The triple Paradise… Oh, Jesus, how good is this. Enjoying body capacity."

Media Guy gives up starting to touch girls. *There is no way out* he concludes. Girls keep on loud giggling all time of this indecent game.

He says to himself: "Is this dream or the truth. I do hope the truth… Hmm, how wonderful this experience is." He makes deep sigh of extraordinary pleasure.

Three girls altogether to Media Guy: "Honey… Why are you so shy? Let's touch each other more intensive… That's the only life we have…Let's don't waste our time, Honey. Let us enjoy stream of pleasures." Girls are bursting in laughter.

Media Guy happy about that: "I agree, heartbreakers. I'll do my best. Let's live the only life… Not timing boredom days… Yopie!!!

Touching and caressing get very intensive all bodies of girls and him are merged with themselves in one form – erotic shame. Obviously it gets some kind of quarter group sex.

Nightmare
Clear night, somewhere in the jungle on unknown location. Media Guy stands tied to small tree in the center of circle, made by savages who perform a rite singing strange religious song. Actually, it's wild, wild cry rather than song. Savages are almost naked with small skirts made of leaves. Their black thin bodies are painted in various colors. In outer space, behind the savages' circle head of the tribe is sitting on the ground with couple of advisors chatting. Chilling sounds of savages drums make Media Guy frightened to death. He is in his underwear – white pants with blue-red stripes and orange-pink flowers, completely soaked with own sweat. He is frightened to death. After a while one of head of the tribe advisors, savage who looks more civilized than others, comes close to Media Guy who looks as if he is half-dead.

Advisor in very bed English, words can hardly be recognized: "Hello, gentleman. Hmm... Tribe council made decision."

Media Guy looks horrible with face so pale as if he has died a couple of hours ago: "What decision? Please, tell me what decision!?!"

Advisor in very serious voice: "Unfortunately, you are sentenced to death."

Media Guy at the edge of fatal heart stroke, gets furious, loudly: "Why?!? Just tell me why!?! What are you talking about. I didn't committed any crime."

Advisor tries to calm Media Guy: "You are intruder... And this tribe doesn't like... That's for capital punishment."

Media Guy now gets fierce: "Hey, hey! What do you mean by intruder?!? You will kill me for that."

Advisor keeps on normal way of talking: "Okay. You see. Your skin is white almost like mil. We are black. You are white. Your nose is different. We don't understand you... You speak in strange way... Finally, you are not a member of the tribe. So, why should we save your life. There is no a single reason to do it."

Media Guy still mad about stupid statement, very loudly: "Yeah... So, that's why you must kill me... I'm not yours... I'm different... Bullshit!!!"

Advisor keeps calm voice: "Unfortunately, yes... That's not my decision... There is the tribe code... All must obey tribe rules... I am, as simple as that, just interpreter of tribe will. However, you won't be the first white killed on such indictment. At least two dozens of whites have been killed so far."

Media Guy is screaming in despair: "What bastards you are!!! Wild animals!!! Beasts!!!"

Advisor official and calm: "Listen to me carefully. "Tribe doesn't want to be under influence of other creatures except its own members... So we must kill you." Media Guy awakes up, covered by cold sweat.

Chapter 41

Unfortunately, nightmare is pure reality. Media Guy is tied to tree somewhere in the jungle. He is in underwear – pants, trembling frightened to death. Next to him two guards are watching him. Other savages are sleeping lying on the grass. Sky is clear, stars bright. Ten feet from tied Media Guy is fire-delivering light to tribe area. Media Guy has feeling something terrible will happen.

Guards have long sharp arrows and huge axes. They are chatting in very strange tribe language. Sound of savages snoring is combined with sounds of wild life screams in jungle. That makes Media Guy who is already almost dead of fear even more frightened. Another hot and humid day in the jungle. Media Guy is tied and exposed to sunrays. His body is soaked with sweat; bare feet are burning on hot sand. This is very painful experience for him. After a while black man who speaks bad English and looks more civilized than other savages comes to Media Guy with big dish of water. That only English speaking person is advisor.

Advisor to Media Guy: "Hi… I am the tribe advisor. If you face any problem… Just tell me… I'm the only one who speaks English here in this tribe… You must be thirsty. I bring some water for you." He is bringing a dish of water so close to Media Guy face that he can drink with hands tied.

Media Guy: "Exactly... Smart boy, I am thirsty." He is drinking water from the dish like an animal with face dived in dish.

Advisor is pulling back almost empty dish to himself: "I guess it's better now. Water is more important than food."

Media Guy agrees: "Yes... Much better... But..."

Advisor pretends as if hi is worried about Media Guy: "Yes, you are in big trouble."

Media Guy surprised and afraid: "What do you mean?!? Hmm, I am in big trouble. What trouble?"

Advisor gets more official trying to explain him: "The tribe rules are very severe... Very cruel indeed...Even bizarre in your opinion...Unfortunately, you are here in this area under the tribe jurisdiction. You are not the tribe member... Therefore you are guilty. Very guilty. Not belong to the tribe is crime. Serious crime."

Media Guy even more frightened and confused: "I am not the tribe member... Shit... So what!!! That's not any crime."

Advisor explains Media Guy: "Maybe in your country. But here... Unfortunately, That is the crime... Serious crime. Yes. You are sentenced to death... I have done my best to reduce this punishment - I suggested cutting hand or leg for instance... But, no use... Head of the tribe standpoint is only killing."

Media Guy gets furious, although frightened: "Why!?! Why, for Christ sake?!? What is the verdict?"

Advisor official and calm: "Verdict... Hmm, you are American... That's quiet enough to be sentenced to death... How cannot understand that?"

Media Guy makes ear breaking painful scream: "Shit!!! Bastards!!! Damned crooks. What have I done to you mother fuckers."

Advisor with official smile: "Please, do not talk such dirty words, please... They don't understand you... But they really hate you tremendously... This is primitive man-eating tribe... in other words cannibals... Despite that fact tribe has its own code."

Media Guy cannot understand codes of primitive savages, furious: "What... Fucking animals... Sorry, fucking cannibals!!!"

Advisor continues: "Yeah. However at this point you are under the tribe jurisdiction...They hate Americans so much they won't eat them even in the case of starving to death... Americans are adherent to money... Tribe is adherent to principles... Unfortunately for your case. There is no US Embassy, nor even consulate here in jungle. Only wild animals and wild people. Not so civilized as you Americans."

Media Guy ironic for the first time: "Fantastic... How lucky I am... So circumstances are more favorable... They will kill me but I won't be their meal... Am I supposed to be happy? Bullshit!"

Three young black savage women, almost nude in small slips made of leaves came close to Media Guy starting touching him. They look at him as if he is world miracle.

Advisor now less official smiling: "Don't get angry... White man are not frequent happenings here... You are, I must say, some kind of miracle...So tribe girls are eager to get familiar with you in details." He bursts in laughter. Intensive touching gets indecent forms. Three savage girls touch all parts of Media Guy body. He barely can stand such behavior, in particular, with hands tied.

Media Guy makes cheerful face, starts laughing due to intensive tickling: "D... Doo.... Don't do it... Please, don't do it! I can't stand that tickling... Please, tell me what do you want... Ha, ha, ha." To himself *This is not bad. Some kind of erotic digital games as last will.* Girls keep on intensive touching as well as rubbing their bodies to Media Guy body... It looks like an orgy.

"Ha, ha, ha...What do you want!?! Sex... Or... Of course you want pure, wild sex... Okay, let's go! I'm ready. Probably last time in my life. Come on." Media Guy says and bursts in laughter as if he gets crazy.

Chapter 42

Rescue Operation is in progress. Head of the tribe and Advisor in the role of translator talk to tied Media Guy. "Killing Ritual" is about to begin. Members of thee tribe, painted in war colors, circle tied Media Guy, starting playing "Killing Game". Savages are jumping and screaming in the circle in which center is sacrifice – Media Guy tied to some kind of exotic jungle tree. Their screams are horrible. Ten to fifteen feet from "Killing Game" circle ten savages are playing drums. Death Ritual is about to come. Day is sunny. Tied Media Guy is half-dead but still alive. But it's unknown how long he will stay alive.

Head of tribe, funny, fat black man with strange horns on the head, body painted in various colors. He speaks to Media Guy tribe language, then stops waiting for Advisor translation, some sort of consecutive translation in last minutes of Media Guy life.

Advisor to Media Guy: "Yeah… No way out… Your death is a must… But… Due to courtesy and kindness of the Head of the Tribe… You are given an opportunity to choose the way of killing. That's very rare that Head of tribe shows such generosity."

Media Guy keeps sarcastic way, he thinks it's better than be humble to these idiots: "Shit… How kind of him! Bastard! To choose type of killing. What do you think I am. Bloody mother fuckers."

Fortunately, Head of the tribe does not understand English. He starts speaking and looking at Media Guy; then again after a while he stops waiting for Advisor translation.

Advisor explains "offered choice" to Media Guy: "Now, gentleman. Listen to me carefully. You have several "death options". You are supposed to pick up one...Just one... Otherwise. Hmm. You'll die in boiling water. They will cook you." He is very loud as if he gets angry: "Is that clear to you. Understand!"

Media Guy is sarcastic: "Great! Cooking in boiling water. Shit! Please, tell me what are the merciful options!?! Maybe let crocodile or tiger to eat me, or let venomous snakes or bugs on me."

Advisor to Media Guy: "Yeah. You are right to some extent. Animals are other options...First – Poisonous snakes; Second – Poisonous insects... Third – Water option, to finish as crocodile meal... Fourth – Landscape option; to become a meal of some beast, tiger, for instance... And finally to be killed by poisonous arrow from tribe hunters... So... That would be all we can offer you... It's up to you to make selection that is appropriate to you. If you wish."

Media Guy furious and frightened: "It's up to me! You say it's up to me. Sons of bitches, it's my choice, isn't it, mother fuckers!" He bursts in sudden crying. At that point sound of helicopters is heard. Tribe members get worried but for Media Guy it's happy sign. The more loud helicopters' sound becomes the more confused and frightened savages are. Seeing small police helicopters on the sky savages start running and screaming. Now they are frightened to death not Media Guy. He starts cheerful smiling. Shortly after helicopters appeared on the sky,

Media Guy stays alone still tied but happy. Tribe of savages, as simple as that, has just vanished. One helicopter stops in the air starting floating about 50 feet above Media Guy head. Soon two commandos come down along special rope thrown out of the helicopter. They are in black uniforms wearing masks.

Reaching ground two commandos are about 20 feet from Media Guy. Then they come to him starting to untie him.

Media Guy seeing saviors is happy as never so far: "Hi, friends! You save my life… My dear saviors. Yoppieee!!!" Two commandos are smiling executing final phase of rescue operation. Commandos are untying Media Guy. Sounds of helicopters' engines are still heard.

Chapter 43

Editorial Office – USFTV; there are many journalists and other broadcasting staff. Atmosphere is working; almost all people are very busy. Media Guy enters the Editorial Office. At that point exclamation of surprise and happiness resounds through the office: "Yoppiee... Our Hero has just come! Media Guy is with us again."

Media Guy with genuine happy smile: "Hi, friends... It's great pleasure to work with such colleagues."

Colleague 1, slim mid-aged man with glasses: "Oh, no... Don't do it... Please, no heartbreaking stories."

Blonde lady comes close to Media Guy taking his left arm in her arm: "Why not. He is real hero. Brave man. We should be proud of him."

Colleague 2, young elegant man as if he denies: "Oh, no... He just has incredible luck... Hmm... He is like a cat. He has nine lives. We are not so lucky."

Brunette lady comes to Media Guy taking his right arm in her arm. Two beautiful ladies now capture Media Guy. He feels good.

"Oh, no... You are jealous of him." Brunette lady says looking at Media Guy gently as if she fell in love with him.

She says to other male journalists: "Most of you wouldn't even dare to go where he goes as if it's ordinary shopping mall."

Exclamation of harsh disagreement resounds through the office: "OH, NOO... THAT'S NOT THE TRUE"! It seems that from now on all men in Editorial Office are against Media Guy.

Blonde lady holding Media Guy left arm in her arm tighter: "Yes!!! That's true. Where are you? Heroes. Between superstar ladies' legs. People are fed up of night club reports... sexual life... Fucking and menstruation frequency of celebrities... and other bullshit. This Guy is always ready...ready to go in the heart of the fire...or flood... or to talk to person who wants to commit suicide. And you. What about you?!?"

All members of ladies staff greet this statement by loud exclamation: "Yeeaahh! He is the hero! Real hero. He is the best!... The only real, genuine man in the Editorial Office!"

Media Guy tries to reduce raising tensions, loudly to all: "Hey, hey! Please. Stop all of you. Stop quarrelling. Let's make friendly atmosphere. We are colleagues, not enemies. I hope you feel like eating pizzas."

Cheerful exclamation of approval both from male and female staff resounds the office: "YEAH! Do it. Just do it!"

Media Guy cheerful: "Okay... I'm going to order it right now."

Chapter 44

Media Guy is in his parents home at dinner. As usual on the table are favorite Media Guy dishes like fruit cake and chops with smashed potatoes. Mother, father and Media Guy are sitting at the dinning table eating soup. His parents are very proud of him. But, father behaves as if he is ill tempered.

Father to Media Guy surly: "Yeah... You are promoted... Well. Hmm. So what."

Media Guy while eating hot soup, sharply replies: "Yes... I am promoted... So what my dear father?"

Father keeps on surly way of talking: "Okay... So it, probably, means you are better paid."

Media Guy approves his father statement: "Yeah... Exactly. It means I am better paid. You are quiet right."

Father sharply continues: "Great... May I ask you something!?! One question. I guess it's not too much."

Media Guy sharply replies accepting unpleasant wa of dialogue: "Why not. This is free country. You can ask whatever you want. I will answer all I know."

Father eager to ask the question continues: "Yes... The question is. Listen to me carefully and answer immediately - When will you marry?"

Media Guy is choking up, surprised as if he doesn't hear father's question: "I beg you pardon!?! When... will... I... marry? Did you ask me When I will be married, dear father?"

Father nervous sharply replies: "Exactly. When will you marry? That is my question. And...I am ready to hear your answer, Superstar." He is pricking up his ears to hear better his son.

Media Guy gets nervous: "You are just annoying me with such questions. That's the only you think about. I will marry one day in future. Maybe near. When that day comes it comes.Shit."

Media Guy to mother: "Sorry, for dirty words. But father really tortures me with such questions."

Father sharply to Media Guy: "Do you, maybe, think you are too young... When I was your age you were eighteen... Hmm... Yes, you were eighteen, my dear son."

Media Guy cannot be confused by his father's statements: "Yes. But that's all you have done in your life so far. My job is exceptional. My career is something special... And. Besides that... I want to be one of the top ranked journalists. That's very important to me. The most important. That's my life, not yours, dear father."

Father rather disappointed by his son answer: "I see. No use telling you are wrong. You'll figure out very, very soon that life is empty without family. But, then could be very late... Yeah, son of mine. Do it. Do whatever you want. You are an adult, not kid." Father makes deep sigh usual for disappointed person.

Mother is trying to shift talks to other topic: "Let's do more cheerful things. Put aside hard talk at this point."

Father to mother: "Yes... Let's do... Like what? Isn't this important?"

Mother is smiling: "Yes it is. But there are more important things in our life. Like eating, for instance. Dishes are still warm... But won't last. Go on, Let's focus attention to meal not life philosophy." All start smiling and eating well-prepared dishes.

Chapter 45

Clear sky could be seen through opened window; Media Guy is sleeping in his apartment. Judging by thin smile he has nice dreams. Close shot of Media Guy sleeping. Suddenly his face gets painful grimace. Media Guy starts some kind of moaning. Drops of sweat appear on his face and neck. At this point he has nightmare for sure.

Nightmare. Media Guy tied to the tree, somewhere in the jungle. Dark night; full moon in the sky. There is a big orange flame about 10 feet from here. Horrible drum sounds are heard in background. Media Guy is frightened to death, his face dead pale, body trembling soaked with sweat. Suddenly a savage, witch doctor emerges from the darkness of jungle. Media Guy has a feeling something horrible will happen. Black and fat Witch doctor in multi-color skirt made of leaves is approaching slowly to Media Guy. Media Guy sees a skull in his right hand. Shortly after seeing the skull Media Guy notices some letters engraved in it. He can't figure out what is engraved until Witch doctor comes close to him. Media Guy is really horror-struck when sees "Media Guy" engraved.

Witch doctor with deep voice as if comes from far away: "You... You are the next. Prepare yourself."

Media Guy cries trying to free himself; but no use his hands are tied to tree. Bloody scratches appear on part of his tied hands.

"No!!! No!!! I want to live!!! I must live!!! Bloody bastards!!!" Media Guy cries.

Witch doctor with wide sarcastic smile showing human skull in his right hand: "Yes. This is your skull... Do you see what's engraved? Come closer." He is pointing at engraved letters.

Media Guy frightened to death: "Yeah... I do see. I see very clear... Media Guy is engraved... Bastards!!! You mother fuckers."

Witch doctor keep on sarcastic communication: "Exactly. Media Guy. Could you even make out you are dead... Just imagine it... Try it. Imagination is not painful."

He caresses the skull holding it tightly in his right hand.

Media Guy cries as loud as he can: "Nooo!!! I'm not dead!!! I am alive!!! I'll stay alive!!!" At that point Media Guy awakes up. He is covered by sweat due to nightmare.

Chapter 46

Small modern cafeteria in downtown. Media Guy and Editor in Chief have fierce dispute. It's not crowded; only three young couples are chatting. Nice, modern, full of rhythm music comes from well-designed white loudspeakers.

Media Guy sharply: "Oh, no... No, no, no. Not in any case. No chance."

Editor in Chief tries stubbornly to convince Media Guy of his proposal: "Hmm... No, no, no. Jesus, why not. Am I supposed to explain it."

Media Guy nervous, sharply replies: "No. I won't go there. You said "Primitive tribes ethnic war". Do you really mean I'm mad?!?"

Editor in Chief official and calm as each serious boss trying to persuade underling: "Yes... Primitive tribes with their wars are in jungle. So what`s the problem?"

Media Guy angry with irony: "You ask me So what!!! Great. Hmm. In jungle. Man-eating savage. You have chosen me to sacrifice, to kill me for better reputation of TV company."

Editor in Chief very surprised with such Media Guy behavior, whom he considers real hero: "Oh, no. That's not the truth... You are not good at geography."

Media Guy confused: "What you are talking about. I'm not good at geography. Oh, Jesus. What kind of man you are?!?"

Editor in Chief keeps on assuring Media Guy: "Yes. You'll be in capital. Urban area like London or New York City. Tribes are far, far away... Believe me. You don't risk anything, not to mention your life." He is staring at Media Guy eyes to sound more persuasive.

Media Guy had very bad experience with savages, still has no confidence in Editor in Chief: "Yeah. Far away. Is it far away enough? Enough to reach the capital by walking within daylight. I said once more. And never again... NOT IN ANY CASE! Bye, bye."

Waitress, young blonde lady with beautiful legs is approaching table where Media Guy and Editor in Chief dispute hot issues.

Waitress is smiling, showing white teeth; to Media Guy and Editor in Chief: "Gentlemen, would you like something to drink."

Media Guy sharply replies as if he prepared text earlier: "Oh, yes. Ice coffee. Cold Ice coffee."

Editor in Chief orders the same as Media Guy: "The same for me... Ice coffee, of course."

Waitress: "Okay. Thank you." She is leaving their table to bring order.

Editor in Chief is losing patience to Media Guy: "Well. In the case of your refusal I must talk to Chief Executive Official. Your salary could collapse... or... you know. Hmm, there are many unemployed journalists. You see?"

At that point after such boss words Media Guy gets really angry: "Oh, no. You blackmail me. Shame on you. Shame on you, my dear boss. Is there any difference, the slightest difference between you and kidnappers. Hmm... I am afraid not. No any the slightest difference."

Editor in Chief as nothing has happened keeps on assuring Media Guy: "You'll be in offices of the State Television and your apartment is in luxurious residential area of diplomats and politicians. You are safer than here. Can't you understand it."

Media Guy doesn't believe, with irony: "Lucky me. Beverly Hills. So I will be as if I am Hollywood Movie Star. Jesus. How Lucky I am." He makes long sarcastic smile.

Editor in Chief keeps hard process of convincing Media Guy: "Believe me. You in capital is completely isolated from tribes of savages. You are safer than me in some American Night Club here."

Media Guy even more sarcastic, without any respect to superior: "Oh, really. I'm 100 % safe. The same was with my vacation. And I've almost lost my head. If it's so nice and safe why you don't go there?"

Editor in Chief not yet gives up, still assuring Media Guy: "That's Top story. And you are USFTV Top gun. Therefore your assignment is TOP STORY. Not some bullshit. We are proud of you. You are exact person for cutting edge assignements."

Media Guy still sarcastic: "Oh, no. I am adult person. Please, do not kill me with those heartbreaking stories. Top journalists. Hmm Shit." Waitress is bringing two glasses of ice-coffee.

Waitress with long official white teeth smile: "Here is your order, gentlemen. Enjoy it." She is putting glasses on their table then leaves.

Editor in Chief as if he finally gives up persuading Media Guy: "Okay. Are you afraid. I see. Please, tell me are you coward? I want to know it, for we, all have considered you hero so far."

Media Guy very surprised but not confused: Yes. I am afraid. I'm a human being. Only fool wouldn't be afraid.

Stupid question. Man-eating tribes war. Am I afraid. Jesus."
He is putting hands on his head as he starts deep thinking.

Editor in Chief makes solution: "Okay. Do you want some CIA and FBI agents with you? Just tell it. We'll provide it for you. But we do must have our guy there. Do you understand on site reporting is the must."

Media Guy unwillingly finally accepts Editor in Chief proposal: "Okay, okay. You won, my dear boss. I am going there."

Chapter 47

Media Guy is in very modern State Broadcasting TV company. Black people, employees have elegant clothes and look happy. Nobody could even imagine that tribes' war rages in that country. Media Guy is pleasantly surprised at high technology equipment in offices. Most people are very busy, just few of them have time for chatting. Media Guy as important guest is accompanied by Editor in Chief, mid-aged tall man with modern rectangular glasses, host who introduces Media Guy to other Editorial staff members. He speaks English as if it's his mother tongue.

Host Editor in Chief is entering main Editorial Office – Desk with Media Guy. He has typical official smile on his face: "Now, you'll see how we make the news…For sure, we are not so good equipped as colleagues from U.S. But we rely on human resources, nurturing great media talents, in particular."

Media Guy to Host Editor in Chief: "Oh, no you have modern equipment… Frankly, the newest available in the market. Believe me."

Host Editor in Chief very surprised, not believing him: "Oh, no. You exaggerate. Do you really mean so? America is benchmark in media technology quality worldwide."

Media Guy is persistent trying to assure him: "Yes, I mean so… If you happen to come to U.S.A. you'll see I'm right. You really have cutting edge equipment." Media Guy is shaking hands with Editorial staff journalists. Long cheerful smiles of elegant ladies journalists impress him.

Host Editor in Chief is introducing Media Guy to staff, loud: "Ladies and gentlemen, I have the honor to present you one of the best American journalists. His reports are more useful for students of journalism than exams at Media Faculty." Loud applause resounds through the Desk. All staff greets American special guest Media Guy.

Media Guy is thanking staff for applause: "Thank you. Thank you very much. Dear friends. For such fine words." Again very loud applause resounds through the desk.

"I won't deliver speech. I am not politician", Media Guy says in speech interrupted by intensive applause.

"Thank you. Thank you so much. You really impressed me with your hospitality. No words that can describe my feeling at this point. Your words of support launch me up to the sky," he says. Applause accompanied by greeting noise resounds through the desk. Media Guy speech can be hardly heard.

"I don't want to bore you. But I swear I've never had such warm welcome in my whole life. Thank you, thank you very much. I love you, my friends." Media Guy says. He bursts in cheerful crying for a while after finishing short speech of gratitude. Shortly after that staff stops work for a while and couple of waiters in white uniforms enter the desk with trays beginning to serve drinks. Quite usual image of cocktail party with guest chatting and drinking.

Chapter 48

Media Guy is working oh his laptop in very luxurious apartment. He creates report therefore he looks absorbed in thought. Occasionally making funny faces Media Guy tries to do his journalist masterpiece. He sits on bed typing report on laptop. Nice music is heard from small speakers built in laptop computer.

Media Guy staring at his report on laptop display: "Yeah. Oh. Shit. That's wrong. This must be better written."

Media Guy is pressing delete button. Last paragraph disappears. Happy smile on Media Guy face: "That's much better. Hmm. Top Gun. Now, it sounds good."

He keeps on typing report; to himself: "America will be proud of me. This report is sensational unseen so far in USA." He makes loud exclamation: "Yippee! You are the best. Number 1."

He takes remote controller, switching on TV and nervously changes many TV channels. Changes of channels are so frequent shorter than eye blink. Media Guy disappointed to himself: "Shit. This is like in U.S. Hundred channels. And, of course, nothing worth watching. I feel I'm in my home country not abroad.

I'd better keep on working on laptop." Media Guy says throwing remote controller on bed.

Media Guy focuses himself to report. His face looks as if he is in great thoughts. Media Guy makes funny faces, sticking out his tongue, picking nose and ears. Media Guy makes some conclusion: "Yeah. That's it. Hmm. That will be the best report on political crisis in this damned country. I need a short break. Maybe half an hour, or whole hour. After break I'll finish and E-mail this masterpiece."

He stands up leaving for large balcony with beautiful view of ocean. Unfortunately, he has no enough time to enjoy this divine sight of an ocean sunset. Media Guy is standing on the balcony staring at ocean as if he is hypnotized. Image is really unique. His face reflects as mirror man who is happy about great view in front of him.

Media Guy is leaning on balcony outside, enjoying very much look at ocean paradise: "Somebody must be wrong. Terribly wrong. What that war. Tribes war. Hmm." He makes deep sigh.

"This is like in Paradise. Bullshit. War. What do they fight for? Not any trace of it, as I see. I'll tell my Editor in Chief I want to be correspondent. Correspondent from the planet Earth Paradise. To stay here for lifetime. Not just for two or three weeks. This is so beautiful," Media Guy says enjoying sight at ocean sunset.

Chapter 49

Media Guy is again in State Broadcasting TV Company; as a very special guest from U.S.A. he got very special temporary office as if he is CEO. Leather armchairs, luxurious modern furniture are accompanied with couple plasma TV's and couple computer workstations with big flat panel monitors. There are several oil pictures on the walls, couple exotic plants in pots, and even, big aquarium with colorful tropical fishes. It's more like dream office. Media Guy is walking through the office, stopping from time to time to see pictures, plants and aquarium in details. After a while he sits in luxurious leather armchair taking remote controller changing TV channels on plasma TV. It seems that he is bored to some extent. Phone on big office table is ringing.)

Media Guy is taking receiver, over phone: "Yes. Yeah. That's me. Big boss. Well. How are you?"

Editor in Chief USFTV over phone: "Oh, no. You are the boss. I guess you enjoy your staying in "war area." He bursts in laughter.

Media Guy over phone: "It's not funny at all. Hmm. Not exactly. For sure, it's not so dangerous as I thought it would be. At this point no war on site where I am."

Editor in Chief over phone: I've got your report via E-mail. It's really great. You are not only top gun journalist, but excellent writer too."

Media Guy over phone, as if he pretends to be shy: "Thank you. Thank you very much for nice words, boss. Frankly, I didn't expect it from you."

Editor in Chief continues over phone: "Yeah. But. Hmm. We need some more pictures. Could you do something?"

Media Guy over phone sharply: "Yeah. I'll do my best. You'll get it very, very soon." At that point some noise of crowd appears as if somewhere very close is 10,000 or more people. Gradually noise becomes louder and louder. It gets very hard to talk over phone.

Editor in Chief over phone hearing disturbing noise: "What's that! Is it necessary to watch TV while you are talking to me. However, I am still your boss. Show some respect, please."

"Jesus, reduce volume! Immediately. I cannot hear you." Editor in Chief cries over phone to Media Guy.

Media Guy is Taking remote controller to reduce volume on TV. But no use. Obviously the origin of noise is unknown so far. It has nothing to do with TV.

"No. No chance. That's not TV sound. I reduced to zero, It's something else," Media Guy says.

Editor in Chief now angry, loud over phone: "Okay, Okay! Hmm, TV sound. You won. I can not hear you at this point. I'll call you later! Bye, bye."

Media Guy is ending phone talk puts receiver in set, to himself, surprised fearful: "What's that? Strange sounds. Hmm. Who knows?"

He is trying to exit the office but about 15 savages painted in various colors, clothed only in small skirts made of leaves break into the office starting to destroy all – cutting leather armchairs, pictures, overturning furniture, plants in pots, even aquarium. They stop devastating process for short time when seeing plasma TVs. Savages look very confused by plasma TVs, but, unfortunately, only for several seconds. While looking at streaming images they probably have thought it was some deity. At that point Media Guy seeing good opportunity to escape and he tries to do it. Unfortunately, it was unsuccessful attempt. Primitive native instincts prevail and savages continue destruction orgy. They surround Media Guy starting to beat him tearing his clothes up as well as tearing off all buttons off his expensive jacket. As simple as that he got in very difficult situation. Savages knock down Media Guy and at that point he gets brilliant idea – taking remote controller from inside pocket of jacket he sets volume to the maximum. Savages become surprised for a moment, looking around – Media Guy stands up running away through office door almost as fast as lightning.

Media Guy is now in front of the office seeing corridors full of savages searching for new victims. To himself: "Oh. Shit. Lucky me. Savages again. In this case not cannibals, but revolutionaries. I do not like revolutions. Yes, I really do not like revolutions! In particular those where I take part in proactive way."

He hardly makes his way through crowd of savages who destroy all they find on way. Their destruction orgy is followed with horrible war cries. Media Guy is scared to death. However, any serious revolution is life threatening. On his way out savages pull Media Guy for arms, legs trying to capture him. Fortunately, unsuccessfully. He got only minor injuries such as scratches, bruises etc. But his expensive clothes is torn on many places. Due to savages Media Guy moving through corridor is extremely slow. In some way he is fighting for his bare life.

Media Guy frightened to death is fighting for his life, exhausted sees on left side of corridor light sign TOILET.

"Oh, Jesus. This could be way out to freedom. Toilet as a way out. Maybe," Media Guy says in rather skeptical voice. Media Guy enters the Toilet. It's Ladies toilet. Three young and beautiful black women stand in front of mirror. Two of them fix their panty hoses, third puts lipstick. Seeing man in Ladies Toilet they begin screaming. They thought he was some sexual maniac.

Three ladies is screaming very loud in one voice, as if they call help: "Maniac! Get lost, maniac! This room is for ladies! Get lost sexual maniac! We'll call Security."

Media Guy didn't know he entered Ladies Toilet. He is terribly confused for a moment. So confused he opens closet cabin seeing black man and black woman having sex on toilet bowl. Media Guy at that point gets so confused as if he loses his mind.

Media Guy shocked to couple having sex in closet cabin: "Oh. I'm awfully sorry. That I'm really sorry. Just keep on having sex."
Black woman: "Oh, don't worry honey. Doesn't matter. You are welcome. Ah. Ah." Black man surprised by this statement glancing at black woman, then at Media Guy. All three terribly confused, but black men continues his sex with black women.

Media Guy exited Ladies Toilet searching way out to get rid of savages. Breaking through crowds of primitive savages is now his top priority assignment. He forgot to send the latest news to his home Editorial. Several times he has been on knees but he stands up again resisting almost naked revolutionaries. He lost his mobile phone fighting his way through the crowd of furious savages.

Media Guy flat out after all this mess to himself: "Oh, Lord help me finding way out! Please, help me. Save me. My body. My soul. My life. Please, I beg you, my sweet Lord. I have no sins. Believe me, my dear Lord."

Finally, after lot of troubles Media Guy enters some storage premises. Finally, quite alone – no savages, no TV staff, only packages of detergents, soaps shampoos and stuff like that. He locked the door from inside. Media Guy gets feeling that he is only a step from freedom but he knows he must do that step as fast as he can. That's real fight for own life. Exploring storage premises Media Guy finds a lid; and is opening it. But. Oh it's channel where he sinks. After a couple of seconds Media Guy has finished tunnel ride finding himself a bit shaken up on wide cornice. Close to him there is a huge satellite dish with diameter about 70 feet. At that point he thinks of a great idea. He remembers his age as student in high school. Namely, Media Guy as a high school student was the best at climbing thee rope in graduating class. *He will be sure from savages at the very top of satellite dish. They cannot reach him at such height,* Media Guy estimates.

Chapter 50

Headquarters building of State Television with huge satellite dish is surrounded with savages so crowded on nearby parking lots that there is not enough space for needles and pins to put somewhere in between. Rebel savages are overturning and destroy all vehicles. After some period of climbing Media Guy gets top of satellite dish. He is sitting on the top of satellite dish still wearing almost completely torn trousers and shirt. That can't be described as clothes. He is frightened, pale staring as if he is in apathy. There are several scratches and bruises on his face and neck. However, he feels better and more safe at that height. USFTV main broadcasting premise full of broadcasting equipment with monitors, sliding buttons, microphones etc. Editor in Chief is getting angry for he cannot reach Media Guy. Besides Editor in Chief in main broadcasting premise is broadcasting staff consisting of technicians, journalists etc.

Editor in Chief is very nervous: "I'll fire him. I can't find him at this critical point. Revolution is in progress. And hi is. Who knows where that bastard really is. He likely he enjoys view at blue ocean. Shit! I shall fire that idiot! I promise."

Lady journalist who is sitting next to Editor in Chief in cute female voice: Chief, please don't get upset. That's not good for health. Please, check your blood pressure. However we could take report from some news agency."

Editor in Chief agrees: "Yes. Of course. It's very bad for health. You say some other news agency. But we have our Top Gun on site. Why should we buy news from some other agency. Hmm. Media Guy staying there is pretty good USFTV budgetary expenditure.

Lady journalist makes thin smile: "Yeah. Top Gun. But, maybe at this point he risks his life, boss. You must figure out what it means. We don't know what's going there." Other members of broadcasting staff are on lady journalist side. They show it by blaming glance at Editor in Chief.

Editor in Chief is rather skeptical about lady journalist statement: "Hmm. I am not sure. Sometimes he can be so irresponsible as a primary school kid. I'm trying to get him through mobile phone." He is dialing Media Guy mobile phone number. After a while mobile phone is ringing. Finally, cheerful face of Editor in Chief as if he gets Media Guy.

Media Guy lost mobile phone running away from savages. Mobile phone, somewhere on the floor, is ringing. One very fat savage stops taking mobile phone. Obviously, that thing seems very strange to him – unknown device.
He stands shocked by that gadget looking at it as a toddler at some toy.
Savage makes funny faces, turns his goggle-eyed eyes, and sticks his tongue at mobile phone as toddler explores environment. Very strange, bizarre and amusing situation. After all touching and pressing buttons and turning mobile phone up down don't please this choosy savage. Finally, he throws mobile phone joining other revolutionary savages.

Editor in Chief is waiting for response on mobile phone, but no answer on other side: "No. Who knows what he is doing now. For sure, nothing smart. No chance. Let's contact some news agency. We'll buy this information. Hmm, although it would be rather expensive."

At that point on all monitors in broadcasting premise is shown Media Guy sitting on the top of the huge satellite dish. All broadcasting crew including Editor in Chief is extremely shocked. They see Media Guy sitting on the top of huge satellite dish. Really bizarre sight. All members of broadcasting staff are surprised and shocked. After a while all members of broadcasting crew burst in laughter, all except one – Editor in Chief who gets furious

Editor in Chief seeing Media Guy on satellite dish, enraged, very loud: "Oh, Jesus! Oh, Lord! What shame for this TV company. Fucking idiot! Bloody bastard! Damn me who hired him. He plays fool of himself instead to report. Everybody will have a good laugh at USFTV. Why!?! Just tell me Why!?! For the sake of complete idiot!"

He is looking at monitors and speaking to Media Guy: "Yes! Exactly. Media Guy you are fired. And from now on you won't enter this building ever. Ever, believe me! Keep of this building, at least, one mile."

Chapter 51

Fired Media Guy fired looking again at jobs' ads in newspapers in his apartment. His worried face and sad eyes are focused to newspaper ads. He feels insulted and humiliated by recent firing thinking he doesn't deserve it.

Media Guy looking at ads, to himself: "Yeah. Hmm. This could be appropriate. No, no. This one is better. Exactly for me." He circles ad with pen.

"Entry level journalists wanted. Oh, no. No entry level. I am the star. Believe me I'm the star with long range experience. Hmm. Entry level star. Jesus, there is nobody to confirm that. Bullshit! I've forgotten my coffee is boiling over. It's emergency." Media Guy says. He hurries up to the kitchen, then quickly removes coffeepot from gas range. He makes deep sigh of relaxation and satisfaction immediately upon finishing this emergency mission. He is pouring remained coffee into cup and sitting in comfortable chair.

"That's better. Next phase is to enjoy coffee drinking." Media Guy says. After putting all stuff in order he returns to newspaper ads. While reading and circling ads Media Guy sips the coffee.

"Hmm, really good coffee. Okay. Let's see great jobs offer. That's primary." Media Guy says with official smile. He pays attention to circled ads "Administrative Assistant" "Entry Level Journalists" "Telemarketing Positions" "Make $$$ from your home" "Ladies Night Club is seeking nude male dancers" etc. His job hunting is interrupted by doorbell ringing.

Media Guy hot happy about ringing due to ads analyzing, surprised to himself: "Who is it? Who knows. Guests, maybe. Frankly, uninvited. Never mind. Or. I'd better see." He is going to open the door. In front of the door UPS mailman in uniform is standing.

Mailman to Media Guy: "Hello. Urgent recommended mail – Special delivery for you, Mister. Please, sign here." Mailman is opening black notebook for signature.

Media Guy shocked: "What's that. Tell me please. You can do it, can't you?"

Mailman as if he want to get rid of boring Media Guy: "I don't know. I just deliver mail. Please, sign here." Media Guy finally puts his signature in notebook.

"Great. That's it. Bye-bye. Have a nice day," says mailman delivering luxury envelope to Media Guy then leaves entrance door of Media Guy apartment.

Media Guy is really eager to see what's in envelope. Confused with envelope in his hands to mailman: "Bye-bye. Good luck. Have a nice day." He is closing the door impatiently opening envelope. Inside is thick piece of paper with calligraphic gold letters engraved. It looks very unusual to him. He starts reading calligraphic text in gold letters.

TEXT
Dear Sir,

We are pleased to inform you that you won the Prize "THE FUNNIEST JOURNALIST OF THE YEAR". The Prize consists of small bronze "Laughing Statue" and cheque for 100,000.00 U.S. dollars.

People vote you the funniest journalist of the year due to worldwide breaking shot of your sitting on huge satellite dish. Prize will be awarded you on Celebration

Cocktail on Friday, October 17, 9 p.m. in Headquarters of The American Journalists Association.

Yours truly,

CEO
Alan Smith

Signature Handwritten

Media Guy face expression is quickly transforming from anxious and confused to very happy person. Face is cheerful, smile very, very long, eyes big and bright. He makes strong exclamation: "Yippee!!! I'm lucky Guy. Yuppie!!! Prize awarded after firing. Oh, dear Jesus I'm so grateful to you. Thank you Lord. Money doesn't bring happiness. But. Never mind, it's not so bad to have money. However, we all live in consumers society."

Chapter 52

Ceremony in main auditorium of American Journalists Association Headquarters is about to begin. There is lot of people standing and chatting. Many of them have a glass of cocktail. People are dressed very elegant armed with official smiles so usual at each ceremony. Waiters holding trays with fine cocktails cruise through the crowd. There are oil paintings and some big photographs on the walls, big thick luxurious carpet on the floor and several exotic plants in pots in corners of main auditorium. Nice slow music comes from loudspeakers built-in walls; atmosphere is rather pleasant. Almost all people look cheerful and nonchalant.

Media Guy drinking cocktail stands alone in the corner next to one of the plants.

In main auditorium there is small-improvised stage with coat of arms of American Journalists Association. People invited to attend Ceremony are mostly media stars and CEO-s with their deputies and assistants. There are some other public figures too – painters, writers, actors, movie producers even politicians.

Suddenly, host of ceremony, mid-aged, dark-haired, thin man dressed in black extremely elegant suit, wearing butterfly ribbon appears on the stage with wireless microphone in right hand.

Host of ceremony holds inspired greeting speech: "Good Evening, Ladies and Gentlemen. I have the honor to open Prize Awarding Ceremony. What is the destiny of this cursed profession. Profession of journalism."

He continues in ceremonial way: "Journalists are being arrested, expelled from their countries, even killed. Hmm. But they keep on striving for the truth. The whole truth based on undeniable facts. They are *alter ego* of us ordinary people afraid to make out good from evil, lie from true. They are heroes, that is something we cannot deny. Further, we cannot shut down eyes and mouths when journalists get in troubles." He makes short break by long deep sigh; at that point thunderstorm applause resounds through main auditorium.

Host of ceremony continues his glorious speech: "The Truth without any residual. Searching for the truth journalists risk their lives. Not only their lives are threatened, but lives of their families too. On the other side politicians, other VIP-s even ordinary people blame journalists and media for causing crisis. Unfortunately, in critical situations journalists are left alone. Nobody wants to help them when it's critical. Yes, dear guests, they are alone without any support in cases they desperately needing it." Again thunderstorm applause resounds through the main auditorium.

"I see. Okay. It's high time to go straight to the point. Let's go to Prize Awarding. I see that my theory of journalism in brave new world is boring to you. Unfortunately, that's modern brave world," he says.

He speaks some new great words: "Yeah. We begin Prize Awarding Ceremony with Prize for the Funniest Journalist of the Year." Host of ceremony is again interrupted by loud applause.

"Okay. You approve agenda. I see your faces. Smiling is therapy, medicament. Each short smile save couple of seconds of our life. Smiling is so, so necessary in our gray lives. Just smile in your offices. Your homes. Pubs. Concert halls. Smile wherever you are. That's not shame neither crime. Five minutes smiling is better for your health than two tranquilizer pills. Believe me. Smile can cure, can make your health better." Host of ceremony says.

"Ladies and gentlemen, this man is the champion of joy," he is pointing at Media Guy. He talks to Media Guy: "Please, come to the stage." Media Guy comes to the stage; standing next to host of Ceremony

Host of ceremony still very inspired speaker: "Ladies and Gentlemen. I am honored to present you The Funniest Journalist of the Year."

He is pointing at Media Guy: "Yes, this man has been meditating on giant satellite dish while just couple hundred feet from him revolution was in progress. He was cool. Great man. Congratulations." Again thunderstorm applause resounds through the main auditorium.

Host of ceremony to Media Guy: "I have the honor to award the Prize to you. Small bronze "Laughing Statue" and of course. Cheque." He is delivering Media Guy statue and cheque in luxurious envelope. They shake hands affectionately.

Media Guy greets auditorium: "Thank you. Thank you very much. I'm not good at speech making. I'm just journalist. Nor politician neither revolutionary. I am just ordinary journalist." Drops of tears appear in his eyes. He is excited as never so far and happy for real therefore he cannot stand crying.

"Let our works talk instead of us! Cheers dear people! Thank you, thank you very much, dear people." Media Guy says to present people in auditorium. The loudest applause so far resounds through the main auditorium.

The song "Media Guy"

SONG

My mother told me: "You must be Media Guy"
My mother told me: "You must be Media Guy"

   In this damned world there is nothing
valuable to try
than to be
Media Guy

My father told me:
"No greater happiness for your mother and me
than to see you on TV"

   My father told me:
"No better vision
than to be on television"

Auuhhh... Ohh... Auuhh... Ohh... Auuhhh... Ahh...
Girls hearing I'm employed with TV
No matter, whether blondes, brunettes or reds
promptly saying to me:
Let's go to beds

Auuhhh... Ohh... Auuhh... Yooppie... Auuhhh...
Yooppieee...
Socialism... Capitalism... Altruism...
Germanism... Americanism...
No... For sure, no any ism...
but journalism...

Ohh... Aauuhh... Aauhh... Yeahh...

I am a star
I am Media Guy
Bye, bye, bye

Table of Contents

www.ingramcontent.com/pod-product-compliance
Lightning Source LLC
Chambersburg PA
CBHW071439090426
42737CB00011B/1716